5/17

"*Disaster Falls* is prismatic, fractal—it proceeds like an existential detective novel, beginning with a big bang of grief, after which the author begins to assemble associations, resonances, and clues, each a point of light guiding him and his family from death to life. The book's suspense emanates from watching the author piece meaning back together, creating amidst darkness constellations entirely new." —THOMAS BELLER, author of *J.D. Salinger: The Escape Artist*

"Keenly observed and deeply felt, this book is not only a powerful reflection on grief and loss, but also an intimately textured history of fathers and sons. An unflinchingly honest, moving memoir of loss and recovery." —*KIRKUS REVIEWS*

"*Disaster Falls* is a father's grief-stricken book, a work of expiation, homage, and remembrance, and it moved me, as it will move many others, because it is authentic, resonant and true, deeply thoughtful, utterly real." —EDWARD HIRSCH, author of *Gabriel: A Poem*

"Stunning . . . *Disaster Falls* leaps beyond death, avoiding the maudlin by turning toward connection. Gerson meditates on how to raise children to be confident, life-living risk-takers in spite of danger, and shares a generous portrait of a marriage in which husband and wife give each other space in grief and love. An astonishing book." —CHRISTA PARRAVANI, author of *Her: A Memoir*

"This diamond-sharp book is both meticulous and breathtaking. . . . While [Gerson] takes us to the precipice of the fatality, it's as if the accident itself is secondary to the larger story. This creates a narrative tension. . . . Though we know the outcome, we hold our breath as he and Owen approach the falls. . . . A beautiful book, even as it deals with unthinkable anguish." —*LIBRARY JOURNAL* (starred)

DISASTER
FALLS

a family story

STÉPHANE GERSON

CROWN
NEW YORK

Published in the United States by Crown Publishers, an imprint of the
Crown Publishing Group, a division of Penguin Random House LLC,
New York.
crownpublishing.com

CROWN is a registered trademark and the Crown colophon is
a trademark of Penguin Random House LLC.

Grateful acknowledgement is made to the following:
Hal Leonard LLC: lyrics from "Under Pressure;" words and music by
Freddie Mercury, John Deacon, Brian May, Roger Taylor, and David Bowie.
Copyright © 1981 by EMI Music Publishing Ltd., Queen Music Ltd. and
Tintoretto Music. All rights on behalf of EMI Music Publishing Ltd. and
Queen Music Ltd. Administered by Sony/ATV Music Publishing LLC,
424 Church Street, Suite 1200, Nashville, TN 37219. All rights on behalf
of Tintoretto Music administered by RZO Music. International copyright
secured. Reprinted by permission of Hal Leonard LLC. All rights reserved.
RZO Music, Inc.: lyrics from "Under Pressure," written by David Bowie,
John Deacon, Brian May, Freddie Mercury, and Roger Taylor. Reprinted
by permission of Tintoretto Music administered by RZO Music, Inc.
All rights reserved.

Grateful acknowledgment is made to the Estate of Diane Arbus for
permission to reprint the photograph entitled "A Family on Their Lawn
One Sunday in Westchester, N.Y." Copyright © The Estate of Diane Arbus.

Library of Congress cataloging-in-publication data is available upon request.

ISBN 978-1-101-90669-9
eISBN 978-1-101-90670-5

PRINTED IN THE UNITED STATES OF AMERICA

Book design by Anna Thompson
Jacket design by Michael Morris

10 9 8 7 6 5 4 3 2 1

First Edition

CONTENTS

Under pressure that burns a building down

Splits a family in two

Puts people on streets

It's the terror of knowing

What this world is about

Queen and David Bowie, "Under Pressure"

DISASTER
FALLS

PROLOGUE

What we came to call the accident occurred on the Green River, near the border between Utah and Colorado. Life was good—filled with its daily conflicts and anxieties and unmet expectations, but good. Afterward, Owen was gone and we remained. Such things happen every day. Accidents, losses, and separations are the texture of human existence. If the circumstances are dramatic enough to appall or fascinate, the story makes the paper. A few years ago, the *New York Times* devoted four columns to a family caught in a flash flood in New Hampshire. The parents and the oldest child escaped from the car, but the seven-year-old daughter drowned. The father could not get her out in time.

Owen's death did not make the *Times*. The following newspapers ran articles: the *Greeley News*, the *Craig Daily News*, the *Denver Post*, and the *Salt Lake Tribune*. Also, the *Daily Freeman* in upstate New York, where we spend a lot of time.

These articles, which I read days after the accident, contained the same material, taken from the same wire report: eight-year-old boy ... family vacation ... turbulent waters ... aggressive search ... truly tragic. There is nothing to be drawn from these pieces, neither new information nor the comfort, however contrived, of obituaries and immortalization. My son's name is shorn of its meaning, its flesh-and-blood content, its humanity. It has been plugged into a template that journalists put together in ten minutes and readers digest in two.

In reality, it happens like this. You wake up one morning without knowing that a disaster will take place that day. You do everything right, you plan ahead, chart the course, ask the necessary questions, examine the situation from all sides. You do what parents are expected to do, and yet things still break down, they come undone, they slip away, an eight-year-old slips away and dies. There is no destiny at play. This death comes at the end of a string of decisions small and large, steps taken or not, resolutions made too long ago to leave visible traces, and behavioral patterns that, like canyons in forsaken lands, sediment so slowly that they seem eternal.

Things could have turned out differently. But they do not. And when a child slips away people tell you that your loss resembles no other. They say that they cannot imagine what is happening to you, which also means that they cannot imagine it happening to them.

A doctor pulls in close and explains that the hurt will last a long time—perhaps forever. A rabbi confides that he has never seen anything like it, not once in twenty years on the pulpit. Friends write that losing a child is a hole without end, beyond the map of human experience. You are living every parent's worst nightmare, they say.

This is what you become: a walking reminder of the nightmare that haunts all parents nowadays. In a world that promises children safety and happiness, such deaths become personal failures, crimes against civilization, an affront to our collective aspirations. What previous generations were simply unable to prevent now falls somewhere between aberration and delinquency. The loss of a child is intolerable and unthinkable.

I had become my own worst nightmare, intolerable and unthinkable. But I also sensed the banality and cosmic magnitude of Owen's death, at once a ripple in the flow of everyday life and a disruption of the universe. Apart from that, everything eluded me. I could not understand the events that had taken place the day he died. I could not grasp how the ordinary turned extraordinary. And I could not imagine what would now arise within our family, what might transpire between Alison and me. We had to find a way forward, with Owen and with our older son, Julian, mourning his only sibling and the parents he used to know.

Two weeks after the accident, I began writing about Owen and our life without him. There was no plan. I simply picked up my laptop one morning and started chronicling my infinite shifts in mood, what Alison and Julian and the people around us said and did not say, what we and others did and were unable to do. I wrote at all hours, seized by a graphomaniac impulse that left me confounded until someone told me that, while those who have lost a parent are called orphans, there is no word for those who have lost a child. I wrote because there were no words. This is what I told myself at the time, *I write because there are no words.* But it was not only that.

I wrote to understand how, despite their best intentions, people end up in catastrophic situations.

I wrote to dispel the notion that no one, not even us, could imagine what we were going through.

I wrote because banal yet cosmic disasters require stories for the dead and the living. When Hester Thrale lost her nine-year-old son, in 1776, her friend Samuel Johnson wrote her, "I know that such a loss is a laceration of the mind. I know that a whole system of hopes, and designs, and expectations is swept away at once, and nothing left but bottomless vacuity." When Alison and I lost our eight-year-old son, an acquaintance told us that "there is nothing worse than the death of a child, and this is truly, as you know of course, a horror story for anyone who hears it."

It is also against such words that I wrote. When our hopes and designs and expectations are swept away, something has to endure besides horror stories and bottomless vacuity.

PART

I

The First Year

ONE

Drew: *Just a quick question:*
What is it like at home?

Owen's former classmates—Drew and the others—
sometimes asked us about the accident. They also recounted where they had been when they found out.
This is how they told us his death had turned their lives upside down. Adults were not different, but most doubted that we
wanted to know or else they feared saying the wrong thing so
they tended to remain quiet. The few friends who took us back
to that moment did so gingerly. They watched for our cues.

With Alison, they saw a distant gaze and hard features. She
did not want to know what others were doing or what they had
felt when we called with the news because such stories were not
about Owen. They were solely about these people and the pain
they had felt when the accident entered their lives. This was excruciating for Alison, who felt responsible for their suffering.

The signals I gave out were more conflicted. Throw it my
way, they said. Give me another vantage point on this catastrophe so I can grasp its enormity. Owen's death is too large to
remain a private affair. I want this knowledge and I want this
closeness. But do not tell me too much. Do not turn this death
into a spectacle or a collective trial that taught us something and

brought us closer together, even if that is true. Do not suggest that your grief resembles mine.

These were unreasonable expectations, I knew that.

One friend recalled that, during her first phone call, Alison had asked how she would go on living. Another told us she was in her car when her husband, who was standing outside, answered his cell phone. She watched him speak and then sob, though she did not know why. These are the kinds of recollections Alison sought to avoid. But I listened because our lives tipped over at that exact moment and I wanted to understand the world into which we had tumbled.

One day, a friend began describing the nervous anticipation that had filled our home in Woodstock, New York, as we made our way back from Utah, but she stopped midsentence because of Alison's obvious lack of interest. I was disappointed. Though I never asked, I would have liked to hear what happened when friends and relatives converged upon our home the day after the accident. They had to respond to a situation they barely fathomed and at the same time handle practical matters. Someone had to drive to the Albany airport and find the courage to face us and say those initial words. Something else: what should the house look like when we arrived? I imagine that this entailed many decisions: where people would position themselves, whether food would be laid out, how bright to set the lights. There was a scene to compose.

I was only dimly attuned to all of this but did realize that people were stepping in and making decisions—they were making decisions *for us.* This was one of the mental notes I kept during the early days, tabulating as best I could the widening gulf between the old reality and the new.

Two friends made the hour-long drive to Albany. It was dark, I think, when we left the airport. I sat in the backseat, feeling already like a passenger in my own life. I do not think that we discussed anything substantive during the ride, though I could be wrong. A haze surrounds these days, with random moments of clarity etched into my memory.

Among these moments: the sight of my mother, the first person whom I saw as we pulled into our garage. She shuffled across the dusty concrete floor with tiny penguin-like steps, ashen-faced, arms half-open. Though she moved slowly, I knew that she would reach me, grip me, collapse upon me. Behind her stood my father, smaller than in the past, my in-laws, my brother-in-law, friends from the area and others who had already flown in, all part of a funereal receiving line that meandered from the garage to the entryway, the kitchen, and finally the living room, a line of still and silent beings who resembled embalmed corpses.

What happened afterward? Did Alison and I sit with one person or one small group at a time? Did we talk about the Green River? Did we plead fatigue and retire to our room? And Julian—where did he go? All I know is that at some point that evening or the next day, lights went up, frozen bodies thawed, and waxlike faces regained elasticity. People began to move, first in slow motion and then faster until they were twirling from one room to another, up and down the stairs, onto the deck, into the garden. The house lit up with a circular energy that was manic and magical, an energy that surrounded us but could not touch me.

Alison and I began dating within months of moving to New York in the late 1980s, both of us fresh college graduates. We left for Chicago a few years later—I began doctoral studies in French history, Alison planned events for nonprofits—and returned in 2000, when New York University hired me. Having missed the early Giuliani era, we came back to a city that was cleaner and more affluent than the one we had known. We had two sons now, Julian and Owen, born three years apart in the late 1990s. Through their school and Little League games, we found ourselves in a universe of music producers, architects, account executives, film editors, academics, artists, venture capitalists, and foodies—all of us wearing black jeans and listening to the Red Hot Chili Peppers, or later Wilco. There was something intoxicating about downtown, a self-awareness of cool powered by a mix of prosperity and faux nonchalance.

New York also felt safer than the city we had known in the 1980s—except of course on 9/11. We were living in a Battery Park City rental, a few blocks south of the World Trade Center and within the evacuation zone. When we returned to our apartment to collect our belongings a week later, the fire still smoldered, its odor pungent. Trees sported white leaves—pages from memos, official letters, and instruction manuals shredded into macabre confetti. A dozen crushed ambulances and police cars were stacked outside our building like metal pancakes in primary colors. We left the neighborhood for the Upper West Side but feared that this would not be enough distance, not enough protection against the next attack.

This led us to purchase a home, for shelter and summers, in Woodstock, New York, two hours north of New York City. We met other urban refugees there, and also musicians and painters, onetime employees of a now-shuttered IBM plant, retired school-teachers, svelte yogis, butchers who also coach Little League, bow-hunting carpenters, troubadour rabbis, and aging hippies who sometimes look the part and sometimes do not. Beyond the facile caricatures, it was an easy town to like. Our house was nestled in a dead end, surrounded by acres of forest. We had never lived among bears, snakes, and coyotes before, but this place felt oddly secure, as if, like giant cotton balls, the trees and bushes could muffle noise and vibrations.

This is where we spent the first weeks after the accident—hidden away. Everything was filtered, freed from the weight of obligations, pity, and accidental encounters with well-meaning acquaintances. Alison and I did not have to leave the house, not even to buy groceries, because friends and relatives took care of everything, preparing breakfast, answering the phone, welcoming well-wishers, signing for deliveries, and making runs to the hardware store. One of them called the local tennis club, where Owen had been slated to begin day camp, and explained that he had died. Others brought Julian to batting cages, anything to maintain the semblance of normalcy. (Such outings left Julian exposed in ways we had not anticipated. He later told us that, when a camper asked if he had siblings, he gave a frank answer. *Oh shit*, the kid said.)

Another one of our friends placed sleeping pills in our bathroom to help us get through the night. Alison took one every evening; I never did, but we both opened ourselves to this spellbinding human alignment, these tiny gestures inside our own home.

We became the silent center of a micro-society that filled the space Owen had left vacant.

The day after our return from Utah, I retreated to the small studio that serves as my office. Bookshelves cover all of the walls except for a section devoted to the kids' drawings and a large bay window that opens onto the forest and a bluestone quarry. This is where I had written historical books and articles over the years, but that morning I sat at my desk to draft a preliminary version of our eulogy. Alison and I had taken notes on the flight home and agreed that I would show her something by midday.

Writing Owen's eulogy was in some respects an impossible exercise, a confrontation with reality that proved so raw I had to turn my back to Owen's art on the walls. But alone in this quiet space, surrounded by trees and traces of the path that quarrymen had followed decades earlier, I heard Owen for the first time since the accident. The eulogy flowed on the page, with ready-made sentences and echoes of his voice. All parents must carry within them biographies of their children, unwritten but available at a moment's notice.

Ours began with the joy of having two boys and the pain of living without one of them. Alison and I told anecdotes about a child who had memorized our credit card number, and recounted some of his small victories that spring. We touched upon the accident and Owen's absence. All that remained, we said, were recollections—and something else:

Owen looked into himself and into the outside world with penetration and feeling. He sought understanding while remaining aware of his own frailty and limitations. He embraced the beauty and efflorescence of life while grasping its darker, impenetrable side. If Owen has left us a legacy, then this is it.

These words continue to ring true even if I now realize that legacy talk is what the two of us needed at that moment. Owen's life had to harbor some deeper meaning.

Alison and I also spoke against anger. We had both felt its pull within days of the accident, and so we pushed back. We would no doubt feel anger in the future, we said. "But not today." An anger that was equal to the death of Owen would consume us; it would scorch the earth and the insides; it would preclude all other emotions, even sadness; it would make it impossible to truly see, to understand what had happened and who we were becoming. There was no religious belief or ethical framework behind our words, just the conviction that once we surrendered we would lose ourselves and lose Owen—we would lose him again. This, too, we needed to say and hear that day, as if to make a public commitment, to ourselves and to the rest of the world. A life without anger, a life with as little anger as possible: this became almost right away our mantra and our daily practice.

The morning after writing the eulogy, I woke up knowing we would bury Owen that day. Every morning, there are parents who wake up knowing this is what they will do before sunset.

I dragged my legs to the side of the bed and raised my body, hoping to accrue enough momentum to overcome the inertia that kept me pinned under the sheets. As I stood up, I wondered how the day would unfold. I might sit prostrate on a chair, or sob uncontrollably, or fall on my knees in the cemetery. Or perhaps Alison would behave in ways I did not recognize. The images of bereaved parents that I carried with me suggested that all of this was possible. After losing her seven-year-old daughter, the friend of a friend screamed in bed every morning. This was terrifying, but her behavior seemed appropriate.

Alison wore a navy sleeveless dress with pleats and a short gray sweater. The rabbi recommended that I pick an old tie since, following Jewish custom, we would cut it (and Alison's sweater) before the services. I chose my favorite tie instead; Owen deserved it. Afterward, we met our relatives in the synagogue library. I felt numb and restless, remote yet hyper-present.

In the great room, quiet but full of static when we took our seats next to Owen's coffin, people barely moved as the rabbi chanted and then summoned Alison and me to deliver the eulogy. We read paragraphs in turn while holding the sheets of paper between us, her hand and mine touching the words. Like a passing of the baton, this responsive recitation kept us in motion. It gave us balance. Julian watched from the front row though I do not know what he heard. I do not recall what he wore either (there are no photographs). Alison and I paid attention to Julian, but not as closely as before. He later told us that, for weeks, we did not concern ourselves with what he ate.

Alison stood tall, feet planted on the platform. At the cemetery afterward, she held my hand firmly. It was a bright day, with a big blue sky surrounding Overlook Mountain, a local peak we had recently hiked with Owen and Julian, climbing past the ruins of a Gilded Age resort that had burned down long ago. The rabbi asked the mourners to create space for the three of us to walk around the grave. Afterward, still within this human circle, we shoveled dirt onto the casket. Alison remarked that a gust of wind blew out of nowhere at that moment.

Before picking up the shovel, she stepped toward the black hole, as if to peer in. I placed my hand on her arm.

"You really thought I would jump in, didn't you?" she asked during the car ride home. She smiled faintly, but I think that she felt slighted, as if I had doubted her strength. Perhaps I had: it was easier to focus on her potential breakdown than to face my own.

At the house, mourners overflowed into the garden. This was no longer an indeterminate mass, but familiar people who held our hands, squeezed our shoulders, looked us in the eye. One of them thanked me. Minutes later, someone else did the same. So it went as the afternoon blended into the evening and the sun lost its intensity somewhere beyond Overlook.

Thank you for your words, friends told me. We came to offer you strength, but you have helped us. Alison heard the same words and found them as jarring as I did. It took me months to understand the relief that people felt when we stood before them in the synagogue, spoke of a present without anger, and imagined our future alongside Owen's. This is not what they had expected. We might have screamed uncontrollably or jumped into the grave.

Hardly anyone mentioned Owen in my presence that afternoon. I barely mentioned him myself; this made me feel ashamed, but it seemed easier that way. At one point, I ended up among fathers from the kids' school who bantered about vacations and the like—anything to fill the silence. I listened, then wandered off. Circling the small groups in dark colors, my eyes fell upon the couch where Owen had sat reading, legs crossed, a few weeks earlier. The book he had picked up on our coffee table that day— *New York Changing*—coupled Berenice Abbott's photographs of New York City in the mid-1930s with shots of the same locations sixty years later. While some spots had not changed, many are now unrecognizable. The Wanamaker's department store on Broadway and Ninth Street—razed. The block-long gas tanks in Yorkville—vanished. The Jamaica Town Hall—replaced by a McDonald's. Talman Street in Brooklyn—now gone, all of it.

Later that evening, once everyone had left and we had put Julian to bed, I picked up the book and sat where Owen had sat to scrutinize the before and the after. As I pored over the photographs, I pictured him doing the same, feeling the force of catastrophic events that erase the past with coldhearted brutality. Who among us remembers Talman Street? And who will remember the boy who just the other day, just before he died, saw entire worlds vanish before his eyes?

The metaphor seems so neat now. But this is what Owen had read on that couch, and this is what I came to feel the day I buried my son, when the fear of jumping in gave way to the prospect of total erasure.

That night, Alison and I lay side by side on the bed. We talked about the day that had elapsed—the day we buried Owen—and moved closer. We needed to touch, but neither one of us said so, as if some taboo forbade carnal intimacy on this day of all days. Our cheeks touched, our lips met, and then we held each other with an intensity I thought had vanished on the river, an intensity without desire but sharp enough to cut through the night's crystalline stillness. For an instant I stepped outside myself and watched our bodies interlock, but only for a moment because stronger forces took over and overpowered all doubling of the self, all thoughts of sacrilege. Alison and I came together and at that instant she began sobbing, quietly but for what seemed like a very long time. It was devastating and yet felt so perfectly normal at the end of this day that I could not tell what it said about our future together.

Is it necessary to say that during the weeks that followed, pain scorched our bodies, leaving us hollowed out? In the morning, I often woke to find Alison on her back, eyes wide open, mind churning. That was how we now began our days, trying to make sense of who we were. Once, Alison said that the hole Owen had left was so huge that she would have to wrap her mind around it in little bits. Otherwise she would drown. Soon enough, we would purge our language of aquatic metaphors (*keep your head above water, the current is dragging me down*), but that day Alison did not notice and neither did I.

For weeks, friends continued to fill our house. They made themselves available and tried to gauge our mood. All we had to do was receive their offerings. This proved easy for Alison, who accepted all invitations: get-togethers on the deck, hikes, walks around lakes, afternoons on the couch. Companionship was the only way to get through the day, she said. Though she did not want to hear how people found out about the accident, Alison quickly concluded that entombing her grief would bring her down. And so she opened our home to all comers, close and distant. Those who gave her what she needed confirmed what she already knew about the generosity of human nature. Those who did not were outliers.

Unlike Alison, I had never expected people to act in altruistic ways. Trust was a leap of faith, more likely to yield pain or disappointment than solace. Nothing had occurred on the river to challenge this outlook, and yet I could not deny that people were now showing up for difficult conversations. This happened; it was real. During these early days, I followed Alison's lead and grieved for Owen in the company of others.

Julian, eleven at the time, did so as well. But one day he told us he did not like living in a house full of strange voices. There were too many little kids requiring supervision and too many adults intruding on his space. "The B——'s, where did they come from?" he asked. "They just showed up."

It feels unseemly and almost ungrateful to say so, but the constant presence of others soon overwhelmed me, too. Our home had become a kibbutz, a Soviet kolkhoz, a collective with sounds and rhythms and rituals that were no longer ours. It was less about trust than space, silence, and the possibility of listening to

myself and perhaps hearing Owen as well. So I volunteered for
chores outside the house and checked the recyclables bin several
times a day, hoping that there would be enough bottles to war-
rant a run to the dump. I took refuge in my studio, looking out
the window at the forest and the wild turkeys that crossed the
quarry path. And one evening, seeking relief from the strange
voices that spooked Julian, I asked Alison for a day without visitors. We did little that day, but it was just us, groping our way
through the stillness and a house that was not yet ours, trying to
sense what it would feel like to become a family of three.

TWO

Michael: *I would like to know in which ways Owen was a nice boy.*

For months, I jotted down everything I could recall about Owen's life. I did so expecting that this would go on forever, that every day would bring another kernel of Owen, and that these kernels of memory could, when strung together, explain who Owen had been and hence what had happened on the river.

There was his fascination with numbers. Owen related to the world by counting, quantifying, correlating—not like an idiot savant, but with an innate eye. Upon waking up, he picked up the newspaper and sat on the couch, eyes half-open, searching for series and recurrences in the box scores. His math teacher spoke about this at the funeral. "Owen was able to see patterns and the solutions to complex ideas; he was able to use the math he knew to figure out the math he had never seen before." For Owen, she said, "seeing new patterns that occur naturally in numbers was like magic."

Other things came easily: spelling, grammar, where to throw the ball for the double play. Owen was endowed with the seemingly effortless ease Italians call *sprezzatura*. The mother of a schoolmate wrote us after his death that her son could never believe he had as cool a friend as Owen. Cool, yes—aloofness mixed with pinpoint certainty about the workings of the world. He strutted in his crocs and baseball cap. Cool charisma.

As I write this, I want to be self-indulgent and fill reams of paper with such recollections, an unending stream of anecdotes about my son. But Owen was neither self-indulgent nor prone to self-pity. I now recall the time his friend Jordan failed to show up for a sleepover. His mother had found reasons to decline previous invitations, perhaps because she worked full-time and lived in another borough, but one day she agreed to drop Jordan off. Owen and I waited at home. When they did not arrive, I called the mother. They were stuck in traffic, she said. Ten minutes later, Owen asked me to call again, which I did. The mother said she was on her way. We waited more, called a last time, received the same answer. I told Owen that this had nothing to do with him, that things can be complicated. But there was no need. Owen was already walking to his room with a book.

I am convinced that Owen understood this woman's limitations because, cool as he appeared, he was beginning to grasp his own. Days before the accident, he lost his temper during a family game and stormed away. An hour later, he acknowledged that his reaction had been out of proportion. But there was no way he could have admitted it during the game, he said. "I seem tough on the outside, but I'm fragile inside." I now wonder where Owen picked up these words.

He understood other things, including the depth of his attachment to Alison, and when she was not around, to me, and when I was away, to the grandparent or adult he had decided to trust. Owen also grew attached to ordinary objects, such as the ragged couch that we replaced one day. He was distraught when he returned from school and discovered the change. It was as if

a close friend had moved to a distant continent without a good-
bye.

One winter, when my parents took Owen and Julian on a
vacation, he asked me whether I felt lonely without them. If I
did, he said, he would draw me a person to whom I could talk. I
think that he would have liked to have such a person on call; he
would have relished such powers. Owen would often retreat into
his own universe, return to check in with us, and then depart
once again. We sometimes found him in nearby but enclosed
spaces: closets, dressing rooms, and bathrooms. He seldom ventured far, steering clear of cellars and outdoor hiding spots. The
spaces he chose seemed to provide security and an opportunity to
grapple with his conflicted feelings about solitude.

At night, Owen never found an easy way of falling asleep. He
would lie on his side, eyes open, staring into emptiness until he
grew too exhausted to hold out any longer. He liked being alone,
but taking leave of the world was a challenge.

At the age of seven, Owen asked to return early from sleepovers.
Soon, he found it impossible to accept invitations to friends'
homes. He told us he had a "problem" he could not overcome on
his own. We found a therapist, an elderly, Austrian-born child
psychologist who specialized in attachment issues. Every Monday afternoon during the spring that preceded the accident, one
of us brought Owen to her old house in Chelsea. He rang all the
doorbells since we never figured out which was the correct one,
dropped his schoolbag in the vestibule, and climbed the three
flights of stairs to the top floor. The office was divided into two
sections: on the left, a couch and chairs around a low table; on
the right, a play area.

During the first sessions, Owen remained on the couch, but

after a while he explored the room, touching the innumerable books, bibelots, and toys that gave it the feel of a bourgeois salon in fin-de-siècle Vienna.

"You guys talk and I'll chime in," Owen would say as he examined a glass fish or a small car. The therapist and the parent who had come that week conversed until he joined us, not for long but always attentive to what was said. Then Owen was gone again, often into the bathroom, which was close enough to the main room for our voices to carry. In and out, in and out.

After a few months, the therapist determined that Owen's separation anxiety had originated on 9/11. It had never occurred to us that what happened that day could have had a lasting impact on a child who was barely two at the time. But it is true that his life began with a collective catastrophe.

When the first plane hit the towers, Julian and I had already traveled north to begin our days at school and at work. Owen and Alison were still home in Battery Park City, eating breakfast. While Alison did not hear the crash, she noticed the fire trucks driving up the West Side Highway and turned on the TV. After a few minutes, she lifted Owen from his high chair, grabbed her phone and keys, and stepped outside. She wore shorts and a T-shirt; Owen went barefoot.

They were standing before our apartment building when they heard the roar of the second aircraft. Looking up, Alison saw the underside of a jet coming in from the south. She covered Owen's eyes and shut hers before the airliner entered the tower, but the collision was so loud that she asked a man nearby if the plane had come out the other side. Throughout the day, Owen repeated this man's answer. "Plane no come out," he said again and again.

Alison ran toward Wagner Park—into the crowd that was forming at the southern tip of Manhattan. People were receiving BlackBerry messages about eight terrorist planes. Someone recited the Lord's Prayer; someone screamed, "My brother is in the building!" Alison bumped into an acquaintance who had seen people jump from the upper floors. When the first tower collapsed, a white cloud rolled over the park. Everyone retreated toward the river. Some people kneeled. A man stepped over the railing, ready to dive into the water. Another bystander ripped off his shirt and gave Alison strips of cloth to cover her toddler's face.

Owen fell asleep in Alison's arms, which meant that he did not see firefighters arrive and distribute paper masks. He did not watch the armada of boats come in from New Jersey to evacuate New Yorkers. Nor did he hear firefighters order people to climb over the railing and step aboard. Because Owen slept through this, we assumed that he had missed it, even though he awoke on the ferry and was alert when a woman invited Alison and other evacuees to shower and make phone calls from her Jersey City home. Alison and Owen were still covered with white dust when they walked into her brownstone.

Still, because Alison held Owen tight through clouds of smoke, amid the crowds, above the railing, onto the ferry, and across the river, we did not worry about him that fall. We did not worry even though Alison was experiencing PTSD—cold sweats, panic attacks, tremors after loud noises—and Owen continued to say "plane no come out" past his second birthday in October. The therapist later explained that while children carry no memory of what they experience before age two, their brains store traumatic moments in sensorimotor form. Without being available for deliberate recall, these memories have an impact on later behavior.

Walking home after a session, I spoke to Owen about the ways the 9/11 attacks might have affected him: the dislocation within our family, his deep attachment to Alison, his anxieties about separation, his complicated relationship to solitude. He said little but seemed to listen attentively. When the school year ended a few weeks later, Owen told us he had had enough therapy. His problem had not disappeared, but he could now make sense of it. He was moving forward, ready for the summer.

Owen's anxieties could have stemmed from all kinds of causes, including his temperament or mine. Some children are more anxious than others, and so are some parents. But in the wake of the accident, 9/11 provided a way of understanding Owen in life and death. Here was a key to the unimaginable, a direct connection between public disaster and private misfortune. Here was a pattern of diffidence and bravado in which he uncovered his fears, wavered for an instant, and then resolved to overcome them, summoning an inner will that made him intrepid though not always for long. If Owen often seemed fearless, it was because he was attuned to what filled him with dread. This I came to believe.

Past incidents gained newfound clarity. During a pool outing a few months before the accident, Owen had jumped off the low diving board and then walked to the highest one, the iron structure that some swimmers never notice and others need to tame. Though he felt intimidated, Owen did not step away. He stood at the base for several minutes, perhaps calculating the board's height or else imagining what it might feel like to jump. Then he made up his mind. A slow but steady climb, a sure-footed walk to the edge, a clean leap. He did this alone, leaving me to watch from the bleachers.

Fear returned as soon as he came out of the pool. I suggested another jump, but he refused. Owen was caught in a web. While he could disentangle himself for short escapes, he still had not found a permanent way out.

Not long after Owen's last session with the therapist, we traveled to Utah. Alison was attending a conference for family mediators in Park City (she had switched professions a few years earlier), and Owen, Julian, and I came along for a vacation. The four of us had taken hikes together before, especially around Woodstock, but Utah's untamed ruggedness and organized adventure were something else. Every day seemed to provide a new confrontation with nature, another opportunity for Owen to grapple with his limitations through a mix of apprehension, hesitation, and sudden jolts that pushed him over.

At Arches National Park, a narrow passage led to a vast expanse that resembled an outdoor funnel. Standing on a ledge, we took in the vertiginous incline leading to the sandstone Delicate Arch, a sublime encounter with elemental forces and the passage of time. Alison suggested that Owen walk down with her, but this frightened him. His back against the rock, he watched others make their way toward the arch. At one point, two teenagers suddenly bolted into the funnel. We looked on as they ran down and vanished in the ochre landscape. Owen then announced that he, too, would make this run. His swift about-face took us by surprise. So did the intensity of his anger when we told him it was too dangerous.

A few days later, we drove to Vernal, a nondescript town in northeastern Utah that our river outfitters had chosen as our meeting place. This was the start of a four-day rafting trip down the Green River. Friends of ours had taken this same trip a year earlier and described it as a perfect family vacation. There were twenty other vacationers—adults, teens, and children—and half a dozen guides in their late twenties and early thirties. Our leader, an athletic and friendly though laconic woman named Delma, welcomed us at the Best Western Dinosaur Inn for an evening briefing. She distributed tents and sleeping bags. For dinner we were on our own.

Like other members of the party, we ended up in a no-frills, wood-paneled saloon with deep-fried ice cream on the menu. Toward the end of the meal, Owen told us his throat felt tight. He had expressed concern about rafting before, but we were still figuring out his anxieties and their symptoms. Softly massaging his neck with his fingers, he asked if he could die from this ailment. There was worry in his eyes.

The rafting began the following morning—a clear and sunny day. Owen and I sat in a raft with a guide and two other vacationers, a policewoman from Las Vegas and her young son. The river was so smooth at first that we could almost see our reflections on the glassy surface. The guide invited the boys to jump into the water while holding the rope that wrapped around the raft. Owen's body glided as if suspended.

After lunch, the two of us moved to a two-person ducky, something like an inflatable kayak—light on the water but less sturdy, less stable than the heavy rubber rafts, which could hold several people. Alison and Julian had taken the ducky in the morning, and now it was our turn. Owen sat in the front while I steered from the back. Though we did fine in the calm water, he grew nervous when we entered a short Class I rapid, with white wisps and enough momentum to shift the ducky from side to side. Owen held his paddle tightly. Afterward, he exhaled and smiled, droplets streaming down his face. When we hit another

Class I minutes later, he shrieked, turned my way, and screamed, "This is the best day of my life!"

The best day of my life. What do I do with such words? I fear that letting them stand alone is to belittle what happened that day—as if, after such a statement, something terrible was preordained. Kids say all kinds of things. When a child proclaims that this is the best day of his life, he does not necessarily mean that this day is the best one he has ever experienced. It is simply a way of describing a mood.

But these were Owen's words. I cling to them, I know I do, but perhaps he did not overstate matters. Perhaps he said what he said because he had achieved a personal milestone, because he was on his way and knew that he was, because he felt a sense of freedom and safety that had all too often eluded his grasp. Perhaps Owen uttered these words because his throat had opened so wide that it took in the crisp air and let out the dread and exhilaration that stand as the impossible horizon of a life that already seemed short and long at the same time.

THREE

Amanda: I'm soooo sorry! I was friends
with Owen in second grade.

The accident occurred so early in the trip that we did not yet know the other vacationers. The policewoman from Las Vegas, the family from Southern France, the girl scouts from Long Beach: all remained strangers to us. We remained strangers to them as well. The only difference was that our son had died.

Some of these vacationers later found Owen's online obituary. In Woodstock, I read the comments they posted on the guestbook. I did so slowly and repeatedly, as if this might help me feel gratitude rather than indifference or resentment toward people who made it out with their families intact—people who, that day on the river, came to represent a world in which we no longer belonged.

I told myself to accept that the experience that split us apart also bonded us together. All I could feel, however, was an empty sense of obligation, and then remorse, too.

July 31
We knew you only briefly during our time together on the Green
River, and cannot imagine your grief and loss. It was very obvious

from watching all of you interact on the rafting trip that you are a close-knit, loving family, and it was clear that Owen felt loved and cared [for] by all of you. We feel some solace knowing you are part of a deep, rich faith tradition and a widespread community; we fervently hope you are able to find some relief within that circle.

August 19

We want to tell you how truly honored and blessed we feel to have gotten to know Owen even for that very short time. We are greatly saddened by the loss of such a shining star.

August 20

I met Owen on the river trip. I went to this camp a couple of weeks after. We got to light a candle for someone. I lit my candle for Owen. I am so sorry for your loss.

August 28

We hardly know you, but the intense tragedy we lived through on the Green River has brought us together. . . . We didn't have time to get to know Owen during this trip, but we caught his sparkling gaze and his smile. We are shattered by what we saw, distraught, powerless before the injustice of this accident.

July 31

We remain convinced that it was not a coincidence that the skies darkened, the thunder roared, and the heavens wept on that fateful Sunday.

FOUR

June: *Do you feel really sad or*
uncomfortable?

At summer's end, we packed up the house in Woodstock
and headed back to our faculty apartment near NYU.
This return to New York, five weeks after the accident,
frightened us in different ways. Alison feared being alone with
her grief; Julian worried about standing out at school; I dreaded
the daily encounters with places and scents that would remind
me of what we had lost. From Governor's Island, where Owen
had run down hilltops, to Harlem's Little Senegal, where he had
bought an OBAMA 2008 button, his presence pervaded the city.
He could surface anywhere, a sudden jolt of pain.

This remained the case throughout that first year, which we
spent in New York and, occasionally, in Woodstock. There were
changes during that year, but they rarely rose to consciousness.
The main thing I noticed was Owen receding from view, ever
further away. Otherwise, the days melded into one another, each
day equally insurmountable, each one overflowing with sensa-
tions and experiences and yet equally hollow. Time flattened out,
which is why it is difficult to write about this year in a linear
way. Whether something occurred after two months, or four, or

eight, has little importance. During that year, everything took place on the same day.

In the mornings, I accompanied Julian to school as I had for years, down the paved alley by our building, right on Houston Street, toward Sixth Avenue. We might talk about his math homework or the oldest woman in the world, who was 128 and lived in Turkmenistan. We both tried to keep it light during those walks although Julian did point out that this woman had lived sixteen times as long as Owen.

After drop-off, I walked to my office, left on MacDougal, past Eugene O'Neill's Provincetown Playhouse, which NYU was turning into bland offices, and then across Washington Square Park. I rarely made it to the Arch without bending over, hands on my knees, stranded among the tourists and college students.

One day in November, Alison and I broke this routine by spending a morning with Owen's classmates at school. "Death was not on the curriculum, but now it is," the principal had told us beforehand. We met the class to make sure Owen did not become a taboo figure, to show that we remained present, and also to retain a connection to that part of Owen's life. Sitting on the carpet with the children, we listened to their memories and answered the questions they had prepared.

"It happened in the early afternoon," we told them.

"We feel all kinds of things these days, often at the same time, and we are not sure what any of them mean."

"We think about Owen all the time, even when we don't know we are thinking about him."

We replied truthfully but did not tell the kids that we now understood what older people mean when they congratulate parents for raising a child. This is a colossal undertaking, with an uncertain outcome. We did not say that, while raising a child

is a lesson in transience—each stage of life vanishing at the precise moment of its maturation—losing one crystallizes the per-
manence of death. The child remains a child, forever so. Nor
did we trot out the line, found in nearly every self-help book for
bereaved parents, that while we lose our past when our parents
go and our present when our spouse dies, only upon the death of
a child does one lose one's future.

I was not sure what to make of this adage. It is true that the
stories that had slowly been taking shape within the nuclear
family are cut short, even as parents come to mourn the teenager, the young adult, and even the mature parent alongside the
eight-year-old child. Still, this line misses the fear of forgetting
and the parent's regret for what the child has never experienced.
It also fails to capture what it means to lose an intimacy forged
in furtive glances, invented words, jokes told more than once,
sightings of neighborhood oddballs whose backstories are imagined in tandem, literary characters who come alive after repeated
bedtime readings, and skirmishes that play out on a daily basis.
There are tacit agreements, too. When Owen got up from his
chair after lunch and stood by my side, I understood that I was to
give him a sip of my Coke. Neither one of us had to say anything.

Owen's death seeped into my days like an imperceptible drip, an
endless series of microscopic laser hits. In the morning, it settled
in the body language of parents and children whom Julian and
I passed on the way to school. They gently bumped into one another in ways that appeared accidental but had in fact become so
familiar and predictable over time that, for parents and children
alike, they were perfectly natural. Later in the day, Owen's death
embedded itself in simple moments with Julian. The fly balls he
caught and the grounders he missed during our games of catch

were Owen's too. Here is where a dead child ends up, not only in the milestones—the first days of school and the graduations—but in the froth of daily life. True horror can prove so quiet that one almost believes nothing is happening.

On Owen's gravestone, Alison and I inscribed: HEAR HIM LAUGH, SEE HIM SMILE, FEEL HIS KISS. REMEMBER THIS BEAUTIFUL BOY. But when I heard Owen laugh, saw him smile, or felt his kiss, I grabbed my face, pulled my skin, and placed my hands on my head. The ache was acute and unbearable and yet somehow it passed, and that passing too proved unbearable.

It was all too much, and so my body broke down. Two weeks after the accident, I twisted my ankle. A few months later, a rash appeared on my chest. Then, in no particular order: shooting pain in the arms, numbness in the hands, twitching of the stomach muscles, pressure on the rib cage, bowel irritation, headaches, faltering sex drive, throbbing in the legs and knees, tingling of the feet, lower back aches so severe that I could not sit on a hard chair. A hernia—surgery. Bladder constriction—prostatitis. Buzzing in my ears—tinnitus. This felt like a constant awareness of nothingness.

Before beginning his examination, my urologist asked if anything significant had happened in my life during the past year.

A physical therapist told me I was carrying the trauma in my pelvic floor.

An osteopath felt "overwork" in my stomach, my gallbladder, my pancreas. She told me that my body would remain in flux for two years.

A back specialist invited me to tell a story about my body—a necessary prelude to healing. But which one? There was a story about the ailments that, however debilitating, diverted my attention from the void I could not face. There was another story about the body that had let me down on the river. A stronger

kayaker, a faster swimmer, an all-around better athlete would
have held on to Owen. And there was a story about the guilt
that, however much I tried to contain it, seeped out like noxious
fumes. In this story, my body deserved to suffer.

On some days, I could tell myself that it had been nothing but
an accident, an unfortunate alignment of circumstances. On
other days, my body hunched over as ache mixed with regret,
bewilderment, disappointment—and guilt in all guises. Guilt
for signing the release and letting him board the ducky. Guilt
for not bringing Owen home. Guilt for failing to uncover new
memories. Guilt for allowing sorrow to overshadow Owen. All
of this was about what I had done (or not), but I also felt guilt
for my temperament, the ease with which I had deferred to the
guides. This was about who I was.

I sometimes wondered if I was growing attached to guilt as
a way of being in the world—some kind of perverse bond to
Owen. Still, I told few people about it. The few times I did open
up, friends struggled to understand. "You are in no way responsible, there is nothing you could have done." These could have
been Alison's words, too. She said she never felt guilty. Her refusal to blame absolved her as well as others. It was the opposite
for me: with anger and blame of others hidden away, guilt had
free rein.

One morning, Julian related a dream in which he had known
in advance that Owen would fall into the water but could do
nothing to prevent it.

"Don't feel guilty," I said.

"I don't," Julian replied, "but Mom says you do."

Having learned about fate and free will in English class, Julian wondered if we could have done anything differently. But

he quickly added that he was not accusing me. "It was not your fault," he said. Again: "It was not your fault."

Julian needed a father who was blameless, decisive, and confident in his dealings with the world. I knew this but could not escape thoughts about the river on which I had not saved his brother. I had failed to protect and might do so again. This is the kind of thought we register without fully acknowledging its existence. We allow it to hang as if suspended, barely discernible but always there, caught in that narrow space between the life we lead and the life we fear.

Julian's and Alison's bodies were also changing, though not in the same way. Having turned twelve a month after the accident, Julian would soon experience the hormone-induced kick that would stretch him out. In the meantime, he loaded up on carbs—cereal, burgers, cookies—and grew thicker. During the first weeks, well-meaning friends had asked him what food he wanted around the house. Pasta, he said. This is what he had for lunch and dinner every day in Woodstock. He could speak openly about what he called comfort food, aware that he sought refuge inside his body when everything spiraled out of control.

But there was something else, I think. When Julian visited Owen's grave in our company, all he could see was a putrefying corpse underground. This disturbed him so much that he refused to return to the cemetery except on the anniversary of Owen's death. Julian's body may have been changing shape, but at least it remained alive.

Alison went through a cycle of her own. During the first week, she did not open the fridge. Within a month, she had shed fifteen pounds. Her features grew tight and her cheeks hollowed out, with bones protruding and hard edges that I could feel without touching. Creases appeared between her eyebrows. Her eyes froze, lost in immensities that only she could see. I had stopped looking at myself in the mirror, but I saw Alison's face all day long, and sometimes I flinched. She once told me she had cried after seeing a reflection of herself. It was not that she hated her appearance (though she did ask me one day if she looked gaunt). She cried, she said, because the face in the mirror was no longer the face Owen had known.

But Alison needed to feel thin or, as she put it, empty inside. The pounds she lost would have weighed her down. So Alison jogged, she worked out, she took long, brisk walks. On cold mornings, she slipped into black tights, a black compression shirt, and her black jacket. She wore black gloves and a tight black hat. "You look like a burglar," I said, but that was not it at all. She was a modern incarnation of the Victorian widow, signaling her altered state by engaging in her own visible rituals of mourning.

Alison said she was tapping the energy she would have expended on Owen; and also that she was tapping Owen's own energy, his perpetual movement and chatter. She conceded that she could not stop moving, but this awareness did not alter anything. If she remained immobile, she would plunge to the depths of the river.

And so her body changed. Her abs tightened, her stomach flattened, her shoulders grew more defined. Alison's taut muscles seemed to limn the shape of her bones. She stepped outside her body and at the same time relied on it as one does on an engine. No need to turn on the ignition: it was always humming. Anything but a standstill.

One day that fall, I sank into a couch and watched Alison circle around the living room. She moved, she could not stop, and I sat still, I could not get going. Like the grieving husband who, in Georges Rodenbach's haunting novel *Bruges-la-Morte*, slowly wanders the canals of Bruges but always returns to the same place, I needed infinite silence and a life of such monotony that I barely felt alive anymore. "Noise offends moral suffering as well," Rodenbach wrote. Alison, too, sought tedium and avoided certain sounds. She no longer listened to music because the clatter in her head was already too loud, she said. We had that in common. But as Alison whizzed by, I could not always be sure that she noticed my presence.

I wished that Alison would slow down and sit with me on the couch. I wanted us to sit for a very long time, until time itself ceased to be and everything dissolved into a landscape in which clocks melt on red rocks—as in Dali paintings and Utah canyons. I cannot remember what I said to Alison that day, but she agreed to sit and listen as I recited poems by Victor Hugo.

I had read Hugo before—historians of France can hardly escape him—but until now I had not paid attention to the verses he wrote as a bereaved father. Hugo lost four children. One of his boys died in infancy; his nineteen-year-old daughter Léopoldine drowned along with her husband in 1843; and two adult sons perished decades later, in Hugo's old age.

His first poems about Léopoldine, three years after her death, are full of retreat, full of defiant though perhaps vain remonstrances against the bromides of grief. "You wish that I would still aspire / To soft and golden triumphs! / That I tell those who sleep that dawn awaits! / That I scream out, 'Come on! Hope!'" The sorrow that Hugo felt was incomparable and specific. "How I suffer as a father," he writes. This is who he was at that moment, and it is as such, as a bereaved father, that he spoke to me.

Later verses point toward some form of equilibrium, as if he had in time found a way forward. "Now that from the grief that has blackened my soul / I come out, pale and triumphánt, / Feeling the peace of great nature." I did not understand, or fully believe, this talk of triumph. The verses that stayed with me conveyed the razor-sharp simplicity of loss, slicing through flesh. "To be nothing but a man passing by / Holding his child by the hand! / Now, I want to be left alone!"

Forty-one at the time of Léopoldine's death, Hugo could not understand why, given his devotion to the well-being of humanity, fate should deprive him of his daughter. Forty-one when Owen died, I could not understand why, despite my efforts to become a fair and affectionate father, fate should deprive me of my son. I told myself that this was not self-pity—no *Why us?*— but rather the bereaved parent's befuddlement before cruel irony. Owen was gone, and yet, like Léopoldine's, his voice still echoed around the house.

I continued to bump against him, too. Eyes wide open, I could comb my fingers through his thin blond hair and then follow his soft ears, his bony shoulder blades, his back as smooth as cold paper, his skinny thighs, all the way down to the outsized feet that we rubbed at night when he could not fall asleep. My recollections of Owen were enshrined in his body.

This is what I felt, what Hugo must have felt, and perhaps what Alison felt as well. Early one morning, she approached me as I sat at the breakfast table. "We will never smell Owen again," Alison said. She talked about kissing the back of his neck, rubbing his chest, feeling the fuzz on his legs. Alison cried and then she walked away.

Still, she did not like it when I read her Hugo's poems.

"You think too much," she said.

FIVE

Zack: *Just to know, I feel really sorry
for you and Owen was a great kid.*

A cloud of words surrounded us during the early months—
emails first and then cards and letters. They came from
close friends and distant acquaintances, people who had
known Owen and others who had never met him. They were
sad, they were sorry, they were stunned by this boy's death.

I've just heard the desperate news.

*I can't even begin to imagine the terror and the agony that
you have experienced.*

Such words told us exactly who we were: bereaved parents whose
misery was so unfathomable that we had moved to a terra incog-
nita, with its own contours and black holes. We were objects of
wonder, beheld with fascination and trepidation. At drop-off in
the mornings, some parents looked at us nervously, from afar.
Upon greeting us, some acquaintances tilted their heads, dropped
their voices an octave, and softly whispered our names. The whole
town of Woodstock, we were told, knew about the Gersons. The
aura that surrounded us magnified the distance from others.

Years later, I showed a friend some of the missives we had received, things like *How terrible, there are no words.* She deemed them clichéd—common, ordinary, terrible in themselves. I understood her aversion to sentimentality, but clichés become indispensable during our most harrowing moments precisely because we need the ordinary in order to take in the extraordinary. To eliminate the clichés with which we die and suffer and mourn would deny the power of coarse formulations, paper over the limitations of language at such moments, erase the collective dimension of grief. Even when we are alone, we do not grieve on our own. This goes beyond the fact that people take the time to write to us. The words we use when a child dies are seldom ours alone; we draw from a reservoir, a finite supply of words that shape what we feel and allow ourselves to feel. I sensed this while reading these cards and letters, which made me realize that we were all figuring this out together. These words confirmed that something real had taken place, something momentous, something that extended beyond our home.

To be sure, religious or spiritual condolences originated in a sensibility that was not mine. There were also messages I would have preferred to forget:

I am so saddened and shocked by the nature of the event that it makes me stop to appreciate and wonder at my own children.

This news has affected the way I love, the way I parent, and the way I live. Without ever having met your son, when I think about him—my heart opens . . . and I soften and become a gentler person.

I should have derived satisfaction from the fact that something positive seemed to come out of the accident, but these words merely widened the chasm that separated us from a world in which other families remained on a path of growth.

Other messages had the same effect and yet proved soothing:

What I want most is to say something, anything that takes away even just a sliver of the pain of losing Owen. Therein lies the reason it has taken me so long to write: I know that's not possible.

Times like this, as I am now finding out, are not helpful to reassure what I thought I knew, but instead present more of what I don't know.

I feel so helpless.

These words gave voice to an absence, a deficiency, a want. They expressed what, in addition to Owen, was now missing. The impossibility of naming, understanding, and memorializing could not stand. And yet it had to be acknowledged. The failings and hesitations of people who confronted the new instability of the world made me feel less alone.

Though we now lived in a world of our own, Alison and I both yearned to come together with others. When someone wrote, "I cannot stop seeing Owen's face," I copied the sentence slowly and reread it. Each time, I pictured people looking at Owen while resurrecting the face I had so often cupped in my hands. We received other notes—about his smile, his freckles, his kindness with children. "Owen played trains and read to my boys," a friend recalled. "Owen shared his dinner with my boys." A mother told us that Owen noticed when her son took refuge in the bathroom at school; he noticed and checked on the boy. These anecdotes revealed new dimensions in the life of an

eight-year-old who had had his own private relationships with
the world and continued to do so, in death as much as in life.

Some friends wrote about their lives without Owen:

> *When I got back to work, many people came by and said they
> were sorry to hear what had happened. I felt very uncomfort-
> able having people say they were sorry to me. After all, any
> sadness I felt was nothing compared to the pain your family
> has had to endure. They should express sympathy to you, not
> me. Last night as I sat at my desk at work, I was wondering
> why I felt so uncomfortable or guilty with people expressing
> condolences. I began to think about how I felt about Owen. I
> really liked and cared for him. He was so good to my son (who
> loved him). I loved the way he was able to have a relationship
> with girls his age and still be a real "guy." I knew he had a
> maturity and softness about him that enabled that relation-
> ship. I always admired that. My daughter really cared for him
> (she gushed about the letter he wrote her). He was an im-
> portant part of her life. I will really miss him and so will our
> entire family. So it was OK to feel that the loss of Owen was a
> big loss for our family too. And today when people expressed
> their condolences, I thought of Owen and just said thank you.*

This, too, I read many times—as I did with those other notes
that simply recognized the reality of the accident:

> *What a horrible blow.*

> *That's a hard lick.*

> *Life dealt you a tough one.*

One day, a colleague asked me Owen's age, sat quietly for a moment, and then told me this was unjust. No consolation, no need to get up from her chair. This felt brutal, but true. Another day, a friend said over coffee that I now lived in a realm without an exit. "Even depression has a way out, but not you." Spotting acquaintances at another table, she rose to greet them. When she returned, she said: "See, I got up, I left you, I went to say hi to friends. And you stayed here, still in your world, wondering how I could have done that." The precision of her intuition touched me, but even more so her willingness to voice it on the spot.

Some of the starkest notes opened onto private expanses other than our own:

> *When my Dad died suddenly of a heart attack my world turned upside-down. And it stayed turned around, but I got used to it and used to being a smaller family (my Mom and me) with Dad's presence always there, hovering outside, speaking to me from inside—paying attention to my fears and my wants and helping me with both.*

> *My brother lost a daughter in an automobile accident eighteen years ago—she was six at the time. It seemed impossible that they would survive it. They have survived and are living full lives—their daughter always in their memory.*

One friend told me that thirteen years earlier she had lost a newborn son, strangled by his umbilical cord. Another divulged that her mother had died when she was in high school, leaving her to fend with a remote father who later sold all of their belongings. My longtime barber revealed that his son had been involved in a fatal drunk-driving accident. For years, my barber had driven hours every weekend to visit him at the upstate penitentiary. An acquaintance talked about his teenage daughter's accidental death many years earlier. We had never been close, but on that day he called me his friend. This must have enabled him to justify a disclosure that, whether planned or not, revealed his own attachment to once-sharp and now-dulled emotions.

I do not think that Julian encountered this, but Alison did, and it caught us both by surprise, this sharing of pain by people whom we had long known and yet, it turned out, not known at all. We soon understood that, while they originated in a place of compassion and empathy, most of these exchanges had more to do with the people who had initiated them than they did with us. People opened up because we were available and could hear them and hold what they had been holding for so long. We did not have to say much.

This power, which I had not wielded before, seemed undeserved; sometimes, it left me drained or hankering for Owen, who was absent from these stories. But we also discovered things we had never noticed: layers of hurt, gaping absences, traumas that had yet to heal, the tragedy that sits just below the surface, visible only to those who look or know where to look, or at least suspect that what one sees at first glance is not all there is.

Every day was now spent immersed in unseen depths of suffering. Sometimes it came to me through such exchanges and sometimes I sought it out. Reading the newspaper, I gravitated to human interest stories about disastrous events in which everything had gone wrong: a woman killed by a loose brick, a spectator run over during a bicycle race, a boat lost at sea, and of course children who had drowned in pools and lakes and oceans. These were real human beings, not mere anecdotes. I yearned for company in my desolation, and for this reason awaited the calamities that would befall other people. These people should not be friends or relatives, but neither should they be celebrities, since excessive distance prevented true identification. I was after three or four degrees of separation: people from the same background, whom I may have seen from afar or met at a function or *could* have known before they took my place in the spotlight of misfortune. Others would now use their name instead of mine as an injunction to hug their children a little tighter in the evening.

For instance: the Upper East Side father who was swept into the ocean with his seven-year-old daughter as they watched a hurricane from a cliff in Maine. He survived, but she did not. For a few days, I read all the articles I could find about this family, gauging where this man and his wife stood on the ladder of suffering that I constantly updated in my head. Bereaved parents were ranked according to their age, marital status (better to have a spouse), number of children, and the circumstances of their child's death. Some categories were toss-ups: losing a young child was worse than losing an older one because there are so many things this kid did not get to do, but it was better because the child's full personality still had not expressed itself. My calculations always kept me off the bottom rung, allowing me to believe that I was not experiencing the worst torment in the world. But this lasted only a short while. Soon enough, I realized that the Upper East Side father might place me at the bottom of his own ladder. There were no winners in this game.

Other sections of the newspaper no longer made sense—for instance the *New York Times'* weekly feature about a New Yorker's Sunday routine. Written in the present tense, this series suggests that all Sundays resemble one another—that life proceeds without catastrophic disruption from one tranquil weekend to the next. Once upon a time, Alison and I had come to New York to partake in this fantasy world of organic markets, neighborhood joints, afternoon outings to the park, and fulfilling careers. That was the routine to which we had aspired.

Now, my thoughts went to New Yorkers for whom Sundays were days of agony, those who did not even notice that Sunday had arrived, and others who, unable to leave the house, whiled the hours away on a couch as they waited for the day to end. And also those who could not stay put. I wanted to learn about the aimless wanderings of New Yorkers who had never done anything aimlessly before but now found the streets more welcoming than their homes. These men and women scanned the faces of passers-by because they knew that at any point in time other people were adrift, on Sundays as on every other day.

I, too, now scanned faces while wandering the streets: Houston and Varick, Canal and the Bowery, sometimes up and down Hudson River Park although it was not easy to walk alongside water. The first months of grief were about retreating and at the same time opening up to the sorrow of a world that was both shrinking and expanding. It was about pain that seemed without equal and equals who had previously seemed without pain. Neither was true, and this sudden awareness, this unrelenting communion proved piercing and awe-inspiring. People showed me things they had kept hidden, and I did the same. Raw intimacy was the only admissible currency. Anything less was an offense to Owen.

A few friends—smart, sophisticated, sensitive—were too bereft to say anything. Some did not call or write because they feared catching us unprepared or felt that they had nothing hopeful to offer. I recalled my own ill-chosen words after the death of a family friend two decades earlier. I had told his sister that their mother must have been devastated, to which she had slowly replied: "We—all—are." So I could understand why people said as little as possible, and nodded when a friend told me that if he and others did not bring Owen up, it was because they feared saying the wrong thing. "You've thought of this, right?" my friend said.

On some days, I told people they could simply ask how I was doing *that day*. That was a question I could answer. On others, I cast myself as the magnanimous party who, from his daily encounters with suffering, had learned to understand and even forgive the silence of others.

But there were also moments when my empathy for those who lacked the words or resolve to go deep ran short. Aristotle advised against inviting friends into one's grief. "Unless he be exceptionally insensible to pain, such a man cannot stand the pain that ensues for his friends." Nowadays, friends share the pain of others, and when they do not, when opportunities remain unseized, the relationship is no longer the same.

Encounters with unsuspecting strangers did not carry the same charge, but they could also veer off course. There was the restaurant waiter who told us his special talent was to uncover at least one moment of grace every day. When I got home that evening, I wrote him a letter explaining why his disclosure had touched me at this moment in my life. There was the dermatologist whom I asked if there was anything he could say about my grief. As a doctor, he surely knew something. And there was the long-lost classmate who found me on Facebook and explained that she had moved to Paris after the death of her parents. Sensing an opening, I told her about Owen. My classmate never replied; the waiter did not write back; and the dermatologist looked at me confounded before saying without conviction that it was hard, time helped, but it was hard. I still think of these exchanges with discomfort, the memory of my disappointment entangled with the burning awareness that I had asked for too much.

After four or five months, I resented this constant expectation of intimacy, a tyranny imposed from within and without. I sometimes passed on conversations that might pull me to dark places. I knew I had to return the call from a friend who had moved to another state, but I kept postponing it, unwilling to shoulder whatever sorrow she would disclose, unsure that she could understand mine, and too depleted to rebuild or even sustain our relationship. When a graduate school friend informed me after years of silence that he and his wife now had an infant named Owen, I stared at his email and wished that it would vanish without a trace.

Our interactions with the world changed in another way. Friends now refrained from mentioning certain things in our presence: the layoffs, professional setbacks, marital strife, and separations that make up the daily fare of middle age. The expectation seemed to be that burdening Alison and me with mundane troubles was insensitive at best, heartless at worst.

The irony, however, is that I would eagerly have made these people my companions. Give me your forlorn spouses and divorcées, your damaged and ailing folk. Together, we will create our own ring of misery. I remember the stunned, embarrassed expression on the face of an old friend when I told her that the two of us had gone through so much in the past months. Her husband had left her, and she was taking it hard. The way she looked at me as I spoke sliced open the illusion that bereaved parents could find equals. Alison and I had won the gold medal in suffering. We did not even need to sign up for the competition. All we had to do was show up, and victory would follow—guaranteed.

So it was with this old friend. Standing outside a restaurant after lunch, I told her once more how sorry I was about her separation. She thanked me, but added that it was nothing compared to what I was going through. As we went our separate ways, I heard her call out my name. "Nothing in common, *nothing at all!*" she shouted from her side of the parking lot.

She may have been right, but I shuddered because if there are no comparisons then there is no shared experience, and if there is no shared experience then Alison and I could not give and receive, and if we could not give and receive then nothing would remain but an asymmetrical relationship and permanent isolation. I wanted my friend to know this. I also wanted her to understand that, despite what I sometimes told myself, there was no hierarchy of desperate news. Her pain had its own contours, whether it involved a dead boy or not.

But my friend was far and I was spent.

SIX

Natalie: *Was it afternoon or morning?*

Memories pour out of Julian one morning before school. He tells us that he thinks about the accident every day: the morning bus ride from the Best Western Dinosaur Inn to the Green River, Owen trailing him while the guides discussed safety on the water, the afternoon confusion. Sitting next to him on the living room couch, I realize that when Julian speaks of the accident, he means the entire day.

The scariest moment, Julian says, occurred when Alison realized that Owen was missing. It happened ten minutes after the accident, on a bank of the Green below the rapids, as the rafts and duckies pulled in one by one. Julian and I had both made it to land. Standing side by side, we hoped that one of the rafts had picked Owen up.

Julian tells us that he heard me yell out as Alison's raft moved within earshot, asking if she had seen Owen. Until that moment, Alison still believed that he might be with us. Julian saw his mother's face change complexion and then watched as she jumped over the side, stumbled onto the narrow beach, and ran back toward the site of the accident.

Julian witnessed all of this, but it is the scream that Alison let out before leaping into the water that continues to resound.

I can fill in what happened afterward, at least parts of it. I told Julian to stay put and then ran in the same direction as Alison—up the hilltop, down the other side, across brush, between short trees, along the flat terrain that abutted the river. Branches tore into my T-shirt and cut a gash on my forearm. I screamed Owen's name, my voice drowned out by the water. Nothing, no reply. I did not know what to do so I returned to the beach in case he had been found but he had not so I ran back toward the hill. I did this several times, up and down that hilltop.

The accident had split us apart. Owen was somewhere unknown; Alison ran along the bank and so did I, but with her; Julian stayed on the beach. He was not exactly on his own—guides and vacationers surrounded him—but he remained alone by a river that was growing louder and meaner.

Julian nestles into the couch and continues talking. As Alison and I searched for Owen, he sat on a raft in the cold rain. It had been a gorgeous day, but the vast Western sky now unleashed a violent thunderstorm. Some vacationers huddled under a tree. One of them handed Julian a light jacket. As he looked at the river, he began to think that Owen was probably not all right.

I move close and touch his arm, his leg. He now discloses something that, he says, he has been keeping to himself. He tells us he did not sit on the raft the whole time. After a while, he joined the search and looked for Owen near the river. But he lost his balance, fell into the water, and was submerged before managing to pull himself out. I ask Julian if anyone saw him fall. Probably not, he says. Was he still wearing his life vest? He cannot recall.

I feel a pit in my stomach. The river could have swallowed him, Julian could have vanished, and we would never have known what had happened to him. I accept that things occurred as he says they did, but this is too much. I cannot process it, and so I don't. I offer no guidance, no fatherly reassurance, no way of making sense of these events. Julian is alone with this one.

Alison, too, yelled Owen's name as she ran up and down the bank. She also begged the guides to do *something* to find Owen. Delma said that someone had seen him on the other shore; she said that this is where he had to be. Some of the articles I later found online stated that "the boy was last seen near the shoreline before going out of sight." Owen did go out of sight, but the notion that he reached the other bank and then gave no sign of life made little sense.

Eventually, a guide hiked up the river, got into a kayak, and found Owen's body in the water. As soon as she was told, as soon as she realized that the next exit point was a four-hour raft trip away, Alison asked the guides to get us out. Delma had already called in a helicopter to assist with the search and rescue, but it contained too much equipment to bear the weight of an entire family. There could be no airlift from this rainswept terrain so late in the day.

I watched the helicopter take off without us. As the sound of the rotors faded over the horizon, my thoughts turned to the night we would now spend deep within a canyon.

Everyone kept busy around us. There was a campsite to set up, dinner to cook, a death to process. The guides and the other vacationers stayed away as we retrieved our gear and finished assembling our tent. Their gazes dared not cross ours. Delma alone communicated with us. She kept it simple: quick questions about logistics. Though her voice was hushed and controlled, she held the phone close to her ear. She would speak with us for a few minutes and then disappear.

The subject of Owen's body must have come up, I suppose it did, but I cannot recall and neither can Alison. What is certain is that we did not ask to see Owen. We did not want the image of his lifeless face to sear our minds, which is why, the next day at the morgue, we declined to view it. I watched this strange ballet from afar, a reordering of social and emotional space in which people turned to menial activities and looked away from the bereaved family. There is no reason why ordinary people plunged into extraordinary circumstances should behave in extraordinary ways. Still, I yearned for some form of human contact.

Had the guides set a different tone, the other vacationers might have approached us. In the midst of a canyon, strangers might have come together around the death of a child. But Alison and I also played our part in this ballet. We drew lines of our own and remained within their confines. Once our tent was up, we retreated inside.

The tent was small, with little space to move without bumping into the flashlight that hung from a rod. It was too soon to cry or talk, so we sat side by side on the sleeping bags we had laid out on the hard ground. We sat in silence, listening to raindrops burst on the canvas and, just a few steps away, the growl of the river. This felt like a cruel punishment.

It is difficult to tell how long the silence lasted or who spoke first. At some point I suggested that we recite the Shema, the

Jewish declaration of faith. Though not devout, I yearned for some ritual. The Mourner's Kaddish, the prayer for the dead, would have been more appropriate, but I had never memorized it and Alison did not mention it. We both knew the Shema. As we uttered its opening line in Hebrew—*Shema Yisrael Adonai Eloheinu Adonai echad*—I neither pondered its meaning nor expressed devotion nor implored God to look after Owen. I did not hope or pray for anything. Instead, I felt the enormity of the moment and the presence of untold generations who had recited such words while facing their own tragedies.

Alison took us elsewhere. "It is just the three of us now," she said. "We cannot do it alone. We have to stick together, we have to care for one another." I did not know where these sentences originated, nor did I fully grasp what Alison was saying about the hazards that threatened our family. But she spoke with such quiet certainty that I registered everything she said.

"We cannot revisit the past," Alison added, as if she had already understood that Owen's death was not only an end, but also a beginning.

Julian said little in the tent: no questions or complaints. Huddled in his corner, he watched and listened for a while and then fell asleep.

Alison and I remained awake for a long time. She made a fist and hit her hand, her arms, her legs without knowing why, though she did say she had no idea what this would feel like for the rest of her life. Unable to put pressure on my bruised thigh, I lay down, sat up, lay down again and stared at the minute stitches in the canvas. Every half hour, I walked out to pee in the bucket Delma had left outside the tent.

The first time, I noticed the other members of the party seated around a campfire a hundred feet away. They were deciding whether to continue the trip, but all I could see was flickering light and a closed circle. The next time I left the tent, the campsite was dark. Nothing but water—rain and the river and the stream of urine into the bucket.

We barely slept. Minutes stretched into hours, time lost in an infinite expanse that brought neither relief nor clarity. Still, within days of our return, Alison and I began crafting a story— our own origin myth—about a family that came together in a tent, made a pact, and reached into its past while embracing a shared vision of its future. The tent joined the accident and the river in our new personal dictionary. Alison and I repeated this story to console the people who filled our house after the funeral. We told them that Jewish tradition should revise the practice of shivah, the seven days of mourning during which the bereaved mourn at home under the care of friends and kin. Mourners, we said, should spend the first twenty-four hours cut off from the world. The family that had grieved in a tent, or at least alone, would surely hold together afterward.

When I talked to Julian about the tent a few years later, he recalled neither the prayer nor Alison's words. His most salient memories were of the flashlight, the hard ground, and the cactus needle lodged in his toe. I was so surprised that I asked Alison what she remembered. It all came back to her: the Shema, the bucket, her fist hitting her legs. There was another thing.

"You blamed yourself, you asked me if I blamed you," Alison said. "I don't remember exactly what I answered, something like 'You didn't do it on purpose, you didn't mean to put Owen in harm's way.'"

This, too, I now realized, began in the tent.

———

The next morning, we packed our belongings while the guides served breakfast and loaded the rafts in preparation for the last leg of our trip. We were eight miles from the nearest exit, at Echo Park. When Alison found out that Owen's body had spent the night wrapped in a sleeping bag, she asked Delma to keep it cool. Use whatever you brought for the food, she said. Delma took Owen on her raft—just the two of them at the end of the line. Our trip ended with an aquatic funeral procession, as in Venice but without flowers.

It was a surreal voyage, a slow glide on a fatal river, through the same awe-inspiring scenery, the same layers of sand and red rock that had mesmerized Owen the previous day. At one point, the blue water of the dam-controlled Green and the brown water of the sediment-rich Yampa came together in a striking confluence. We looked at these wonders in silence, unable to grasp what the death of an eight-year-old meant in a timescape of such insufferable beauty.

When we happened upon a rock wall that served as an echo chamber, Alison wanted to scream Owen's name, but she merely gripped Julian's hand a little tighter. When we hit other rapids, with names like Triplet Falls and Hell's Half Mile, all of the rafts ran them except for ours. A guide walked us along the river's edge, hiked back to collect the raft, ran the rapids on his own, and then picked us up. This was not necessarily the safer course since we ended up on perilous ledges, but it kept us out of fast water. Alison found it unsettling that, after what had happened, the other members of our group would run these rapids. Had they felt a thrill?

At midday, we approached our destination. A row of official-looking people waited by the water, lined up in some protocolar fashion. There was the Moffat County sheriff—tall and burly, with a thick mustache—who stayed by our side. I took his card and meant to thank him for his soft touch, but never did. There was a police investigator, who sat Alison and me in the backseat of his SUV and listened to our accounts without taking notes. There was a victim's advocate, who walked Julian to the sheriff's car while Alison and I spoke to the investigator. This separation, the first one since the search, felt like a surrender to foreign institutions. There was also a coroner whose name, the sheriff told us apologetically, was Owen. Standing outside the SUV, he asked us through the open window if we wanted to autopsy our son's body.

Before leaving, Julian and I returned to the beach to fetch our bags. All of the guides huddled by the water, arms and shoulders interlocked. This circle was such an incongruous sight—a display of support and affection unlike anything we had witnessed since the accident—that the two of us stood and stared. The moment they disbanded, one of the guides, the one who had piloted our raft out of the canyon that morning, walked over. He was crying, I think, and may have said a few words, but mostly I remember that he opened his arms and that I did, too. No one else on his team acknowledged that something massive had taken place on the river.

During the months that followed, I wondered how Owen's death had altered the lives of these young men and women, all of them caught in a whirlwind that seemed so much bigger than they were. I wondered how often they thought about Owen (and about us) and also what stories they had devised, about the river and their behavior and ours as well, in order to go on with their lives.

Today, the only guide I still think about is the twentysomething who pulled Owen from the water and gave him mouth-to-mouth. Does he talk about what happened that day? Does he tell new friends and girlfriends? What will he say to his children? I do not know this guide, but he continues to haunt me.

In the afternoon, the sheriff and the victim's advocate drove us to the Dinosaur Inn in Vernal, a quick stop to shower and change before heading for the Salt Lake City airport. The three of us sat in the backseat of the police car. Once we entered cell-phone range, Alison and I began making calls to relatives and friends. I opened each conversation by saying we had lost Owen, which meant that the person on the other end had to figure out whether Owen was simply lost or in fact dead. Once they understood, we cried together, we could not stop crying. My sobs and Alison's melded into a wailing that filled the car.

Sitting on our couch, Julian remembers this as well. He tells us that listening to our calls was so horrible that he covered his ears. As he says this, I remember reading that children who watched repeated footage of 9/11 imagined that each news clip depicted another plane hitting the World Trade Center, another tower collapsing. On the morning of September 12, 2001, the babysitter who looked after Julian while I ran errands left the TV on. I do not know if Julian covered his eyes that day; I do not know if he, too, believed that different towers kept coming down. But it has crossed my mind that, as he heard us make call after call in the back of that police car, Julian lost his brother more times than either of us can recall.

SEVEN

Tessa: I remember at the farm,
a chicken pooped on Owen!

A year before the accident, I walked into Owen's room and
sat on the edge of his bed, my feet on the blue carpet with
elephants and tigers. The house was quiet that summer
afternoon, the kids at day camp. I do not know what brought
me into the room—something to fetch perhaps—only that I sat
and looked around. To my left: the purple Jimi Hendrix poster
Owen had chosen in a music store. To the right: an alcove with a
window and a desk covered with pencils, drawings, comic books,
and a plastic turtle. Across from me: an open closet with pants
and long-sleeved T-shirts suspended on multicolored hangers.

As I took it all in, I imagined that Owen was dead.

This was not an intellectual exercise in which I pictured life
without Owen. Rather, his absence surged through my body like
an electrical current. I felt Owen's death in my shoulders, I felt
it in my hands, I felt it in my bowels. I *lived* his death for what
seemed like a long time though it could not have been more than
a minute. When I could no longer withstand it, I got up and left.

I told Alison about this later that day. She listened and then
disclosed that she had recently woken up in the middle of the
night with an ominous feeling about Owen, a feeling so piercing

she ran to his room to check on him. Since then, she could not shake the belief that Owen would not be with us forever.

Alison and I never talked about this afterward. I think we both feared the power of words that, once released, might act upon the world. Better to leave them unspoken. But the two of us carried these two memories in distant corners of our minds, quietly and sheepishly.

After the accident, they blended into what Alison and I labeled a premonition, at once uncanny and meaningful. This happened so quickly—on the river, that very day—that we mentioned it in our eulogy: *Both of us have always been aware of the fragility of Owen's presence among us. We just felt it, independently, in ways that escape rational explanation. When he was alive, we treasured every moment with him because we sensed, somewhere, that they might not be eternal.*

I could quibble with some words. It was not true that we had *always* been aware of Owen's fragile presence or that we treasured *every* moment with him. But it is true that I had never sat on Julian's bed and felt his death. It is true that Alison had only had such a dream regarding Owen. And it is true that on the Green River, only hours after the accident, Alison and I confessed to each other that while Owen's death was intolerable, it did not come as a surprise. This was not a long conversation: just a few words, a movement of the head, sustained eye contact. We kept it short because there was something disturbing in the idea that we had sensed Owen's early death, as if it had been preordained.

Perhaps it was only disturbing to me. Alison added to the premonition during the weeks that followed our return to Woodstock. She talked about the fortune-teller who had once told her that a life-changing event would occur in her forty-second year. She had turned forty-two the year of the accident and decided to wait before scheduling a minor surgical procedure. Three months later, we left for Utah. On the eve of our departure, Owen had gone into a funk. He had told us he was sad, and insisted upon spending time on his own. His dark moods concerned us, but only now, after the accident, did Alison suggest that Owen had intuited that he would never return to Woodstock. "It's like those people who know they are going to die," she said.

I did not like it when people told us that Owen had gone through his full cycle of growth and accomplished everything he was meant to accomplish, or that he had died because a terrible fate awaited him on earth. But the premonition loomed so large after the accident that I shared it with a few friends. One of them kept returning to the fact that Alison and I had felt something so similar. The two of you knew him so intimately, he said. Another friend told me that it is common for parents to entertain such thoughts, especially with their youngest child. She, too, had gone into her daughter's room and imagined life without her.

This friend may have been right, but her words made me grimace. If my premonition and Alison's were humdrum, if they were not linked to the particulars of Owen's life and death, then we were left with an eight-year-old dying a senseless, solitary death in the depths of a canyon. No parent can live with that.

One of the first places we visited in Utah, days before the rafting trip, was the small town of Helper (population 2,189). Located between Salt Lake City and Grand Junction, surrounded by canyons and ridges, Helper was founded in the 1880s to house railroad workers. The Denver and Rio Grande Western Railroad made it a freight terminal, with a depot for helper engines that aided trains on the steep climb up Price Canyon. This is how the town got its name.

We got off U.S. Route 6 in search of lunch and ended up in a place that was not quite a ghost town but looked like one, with abandoned single-family homes, a rickety bridge, and shuttered storefronts on Main Street. Next to the rundown movie theater, a deli had been transformed into a temporary thrift store, its floor covered with boxes of used clothes and toys, mismatched china, and old magazines. The day we walked in, an eight-year-old girl and her younger brother were manning the store, which belonged to their grandparents. We browsed for a while then had lunch a few doors down, in the only restaurant still open in the early afternoon. The room was crowded, with groups of beefy men at some tables and families at others.

The first anniversary of the nearby Crandall Canyon Mine disaster had come and gone earlier that month. This collapse had registered as a 3.9-magnitude earthquake: six miners trapped, their bodies never recovered, two rescuers and an inspector buried while trying to reach them. The mining company had been fined more than three million dollars for inadequate design, miscalculations, overly aggressive mining, withholding of information, and other safety violations that directly led to these deaths. "Had I known that this evil mountain, this alive mountain, would do what it did, I would never have sent the miners in there," the mine owner later said. Our waitress told us that everyone in Helper knew at least one victim. She said this in a straightforward tone, with resignation in her voice.

Death was everywhere in Helper. This may have been why Owen and Julian disliked the town, why they saw no poetry in the decrepitude of Main Street or the old railroad cars turned into outdoor relics in the local park. They could not wait to leave.

But they quarreled that afternoon, and Owen took refuge on a stoop and then asked us to get the car and pick him up there. For a few minutes, as Alison and I walked a few blocks with Julian, it was just three of us—and Owen alone in a town that no longer lived up to its name.

A few months after the funeral, I suddenly thought of Helper and wrote down every detail I could recall. I wrote with urgency, consumed by the need to consign these events to memory. As I did so, I felt again the presence of those two moments: the day I entered Owen's room and sensed his absence and the night Alison awoke with a terrifying presentiment. Nearly forgotten incidents and recent disasters came together within a natural order that had remained invisible until then. This was not about fate—so I told myself once again. There was nothing predestined, just a story of death and foreboding whose force I could not deny.

EIGHT

Matthew: *What was Owen's*
favorite thing to do?

FROM: ALISON GERSON, "REGRET.O.GRAM"
          <REGRET.O.GRAM@GMAIL.COM>
DATE: SEPTEMBER 24, 2009 11:57:19 AM EDT
TO: COSMICAPOLOGY@GMAIL.COM
SUBJECT: I AM SO SORRY

Dear Owen,

I am so sorry. There is nothing more to say to you at this point. I am sorry you are gone. I'm sorry we couldn't save you, find you, protect you.

I'm sorry you have missed out on life and its many wonders. I am sorry for ourselves, for missing you as a child, adolescent, adult. I am sorry you will never marry, have sex, kiss a girl. I am sorry for Julian. Sorry you can't see your brother growing up, with braces, at his Bar Mitzvah. I am sorry your front teeth didn't come in before you died. I'm sorry we signed up for that trip. Sorry we trusted them. Sorry we allowed you to push the limits. I hope you are happy and thriving and surrounded by love. I feel your love

*around me all the time. Especially when you send me hearts
and bunnies. I love my dreams with you. Loved your eyes in
my dream last night. I really think you control these dreams.
I wish you could reply to this email. I have often thought of
sending you an email—would you get it? I am so sorry you
are not with me physically—you are with me all the time,
every second, but physically where are you?*

*I'm sorry I will not be able to mother you into adult-
hood. Kiss you goodnight every night and good morning
every morning. I'm sorry your soft skin and beautiful eyes
have been taken from me. I'm sorry you aren't getting older,
changing, growing. I'm sorry my life is what it is—without
you. I'm sorry I no longer adore life. Life without you is
empty and I'm sorry to say that. Hopefully it won't always
be like that. I'm sorry I may forget things about you.*

*I'm not sorry you were in my life for 8½ years or that I
loved you as much as I did. I am sorry you are gone.*

Love,
Mommy

Alison felt Owen's presence from the moment we returned to
Woodstock. She felt it when she found a heart-shaped stone
and when a rabbit crossed the road (Alison used to call Owen
"bunny"). She felt it when she accidentally typed *live* instead of
love on her phone. This was Owen telling her to go on with
her life. She also felt his presence when Utah's Wall Arch, located along the Devils Garden Trail in Arches National Park,
collapsed two weeks after the accident. This was Owen's energy
at work, Owen testing his strength.

Sitting on our deck in Woodstock one evening, I asked Alison whether Owen was with us right then. If my question surprised her, she did not say so. "Yes, he's here." Where? "Probably on that log over there." I thought she had made this up on the spot, but no, she had felt Owen's presence before I asked, without having to articulate it. While Alison has never been spiritual, she now talked about spirits and forces. She could acknowledge her need to believe in all this, but self-awareness did not make her experiences any less vivid.

More than a belief, this presence was a certainty that had sprouted fully formed—the natural prolongation of Alison's relationship with Owen before the accident. She once drew a line with her finger from her throat to her abdomen. "Owen lives inside me," she said. "He is in my heart, in my body. He grounds me, he keeps me stable." The two of them had shared a profound connection—deepened by what they had lived through together on 9/11. Alison loved Julian just as much, but Owen's personality was closer to hers than to mine. Alison recognized herself in Owen, and he probably recognized himself in her: the street smarts, the self-sufficiency and natural leadership, the blustering confidence masking a need for reassurance. Both yearned to be understood and sometimes felt misunderstood—but never by each other. Alison once told me she sensed Owen's needs before he voiced them. Even if Owen had pulled away during his teenage years, she knew he would have come back to her.

Alison said that living without the person most like her was the hardest thing. Owen's death made her feel as if she had lost a visceral part of herself. But she had no regrets about anything she had done or failed to do as a mother; she felt no need to revisit any facet of their relationship, or assess Owen's feelings toward her, or examine her own behavior before his death. There was nothing to revisit because Alison never doubted that Owen loved her and never wondered if he had known how much she loved him. Her bond with him was as secure and intimate in death as it had been when he was alive.

My relationship with Owen had always been steeped in difference. His sense of privacy ran deeper, his locus of satisfaction seemed to stem from within in a way that mine did not. Whereas he improvised and trusted his instincts, I prepared and planned ahead. All of this crystallized a month before the accident, as the two of us drove to Cooperstown for a father-son weekend (Julian was at sleep-away camp). From the backseat, Owen told me he would soon have to resolve a lingering issue with a friend. I suggested that he rehearse what he might say, but this held no interest. "I'll wing it," Owen replied with nonchalance and conviction.

Owen's outward confidence matched his fine farm-boy looks and athletic talent—all of which had eluded me as a child. Growing up, I had harbored the notion that some people lived in a realm in which things came easily and life proved fuller and richer. Adulthood had punctured this illusion, but there was something bewildering about Owen, something that sometimes made it difficult to believe that he was my son.

Owen and I devised games and created characters whom we impersonated. He had begun calling me Pops, which I liked. But I worried that I would never understand him, and that he did not understand me. I had long taken on the burden of protection in our family, insisting that the kids hold my hand in subway stations or bike near the curb on country roads. Owen pushed back. Skiing in the Catskills one afternoon, he missed a midslope jump-off on a lift and rose into the white ether, the safety bar high above his head. I grabbed his waist and pulled him down. As we recovered our bearings, Owen told me with some vehemence that he would have done fine on his own.

Owen once called me a wuss, a term that, as he used it, went beyond its dictionary definitions: feeble, ineffectual, cowardly. For Owen, *wuss* denoted a fearful relationship to the world. His third-grade journal includes a sunlike diagram: a large circle containing my name and, all around it, lines leading to a dozen bubbles, each one of them filled with a character trait. One mentions my sense of humor, but there is also "scared of heights" and "scared a lot."

It is possible that Owen once again acted tough at the precise moment that he sensed his own fear. It is possible that he berated me because his fears stemmed not only from 9/11, but also from the trepidation I expressed in his presence. Owen may have felt this without being able to put it into words.

All this is conceivable, but I did not consider any of these possibilities at the time. Though his words hit hard, I wondered instead whether eight-year-olds can understand the dangers of the world. Can they grasp a parent's burden of responsibility? Someone had to look after Owen despite his need for autonomy. Someone, I told myself, had to be scared a lot.

Alison sometimes mocked my protective nature, too. She did so in a gentler fashion. Instead of calling me a wuss, she laughed with the boys when I made them hold my hand as the subway approached. After the accident, however, she listened as I reexamined past incidents from our family life. On 9/11, I had dropped Julian off at school and then spent the morning a mile from Ground Zero, secluded in a small library office whose thick concrete walls bunkered me off from the world. Without cell access, I did not learn about the attacks until one p.m. Although NYU had set up a TV in the library lobby, no one had knocked on the office doors to alert patrons. This made me one of the last able New Yorkers to find out what had happened. By that time, a friend had taken Julian to her apartment, and Alison and Owen had been evacuated to New Jersey.

This became part of our family lore, a story repeated again and again to people who had not known us in 2001. I winced each time I had to recount it, and even more so while listening to Alison's rendering, because I could not tell where the story about my work ethic ended and where the tale about parental absence began. Early that afternoon, I had picked up Julian at a friend's home, sat him on a bench across from St. Mark's Church in the East Village, and tried to explain why towers had burned outside his classroom window. But I did not mention my absence that morning, and did not see Owen until he and Alison returned to Manhattan two days later.

The day's events made me even more protective. Though I now understood how easily outside forces can split parents and children apart, I could not help but wonder whether Owen knew that he could trust me, that I would look after him. Did he know how much I loved him? Alison assured me he did, but that summer in Utah, I was still waiting to hear it from him.

I struggled to uncover Owen's presence after his death. When a friend asked if I felt it around the Woodstock house, in the buds sprouting in the woods, among the butterflies that flew in close, or through openings in the clouds, I had to shake my head and say no. When Wall Arch collapsed, the only thing I thought about was ephemerality and fragility behind strength. I could not fathom what the Buddhist monk Thích Nhất Hanh meant when he declared that "to say that he no longer exists is just an imaginary construction of our discriminative mind. If we know how to look deeply, we will be able to perceive his presence." Somebody sent me this quotation. All I understood was that there was a way and that it escaped me.

It was not for want of trying. Within two weeks of the funeral, I had devised a morning ritual, an incantation that I recited in order to somehow exist without but also with Owen. It included the Kaddish, which I read in Hebrew for the cadence of the words; a list of Owen's qualities; bromides such as "Take the risk that people are good"; and summons to both love Julian unconditionally and listen to Alison's pain. There was also a quotation from Carlos Fuentes, who lost two children, about coping by bringing the person one loves inside oneself. I read this quotation every morning and hoped to one day understand it.

Once or twice, I repeated Owen's name like a mantra—a trance-like litany with the soft *n* slipping into the open *o*: Owen Owen Owen Owen Owenowenowenowen. I recalled the different ways in which we had pronounced the name. The two-syllable *Ow–en* when we played hide-and-seek . . . The accent on the *o* when we went looking for him: *O*-wen? . . . The low-pitched, extended *n*—which became almost its own syllable—when he pushed the limits . . . The doubling of the final syllable when he impressed us: *Owen-en.*

One morning, I filled a sheet of paper with his name, over and over again, line after line, until no space remained.

Owen Owen Owen Owen Owen Owen Owen Owen Owen Owen
Owen Owen Owen Owen Owen Owen Owen Owen Owen Owen
Owen Owen Owen Owen Owen Owen Owen Owen Owen Owen
Owen Owen Owen Owen Owen Owen Owen Owen Owen Owen

The mantra was not only meditation, but also penitence and punishment, as if incessant writing could express contrition.

I made lists of things Owen had liked and disliked. I collected memories—sentimental, humdrum, tactile. I sometimes leaned toward memories of strife because I found it easier to mourn a difficult or tortured child rather than one who enjoyed all facets of life. Grief can be ruthless that way. I went about this task feverishly, convinced that, unless I transcribed these memories as soon as they surfaced, they would melt, they would vanish, Owen would melt and vanish.

By the fourth month, I could no longer come up with a new memory every day, and soon not every other day either. I thought I had exhausted the reserve, but there was still a trickle, a last spurt. And then that was it: no more memories. "All of these things have passed like shadow and wind!" Victor Hugo wrote. This was the total of Owen. I hoped it was not the end of Owen.

Around that time, I visited his grave on my own for the first time. It was a gray, wispy November day with a wet sky. Having parked near his plot, I looked around the car for a piece of candy to bring to Owen, but there was none so I placed a pebble by his engraved name (following Jewish custom) and told myself that he deserved better than this. Dead leaves had accumulated on the gravestone. I thought about removing them, but it began to drizzle so I drove away.

Owen had to be elsewhere. Back in New York City, I left our apartment one morning with a camera to photograph places that had mattered to him, places that might retain a trace of his presence. I wanted to do so before our neighborhood no longer resembled the one he had known. Our building's lobby, with the granite bench on which he sometimes rested after playing outside. The concrete ball field at Houston and Sixth Avenue where, standing behind the fence, Alison and I once watched him take the quarterback position as if it belonged to him. The stoop of his school on Bleecker Street, where he waited to be picked up in the afternoon. The Italian barbershop on Thompson, where he sat among Village locals and college students. The J. J. Walker Park on Hudson, where he watched Julian belt hits during Little League season.

I also took a picture of the child therapist's office on the day Alison and I walked up the three flights of stairs and told her Owen had died.

I planned to resume this project another day—my list contained locations in other neighborhoods—but I never did. In fact, I only looked at these photographs on one occasion, and never showed them to anyone, not even to Alison. All I could see was Owen's absence, empty space, and ghostly shadows.

Could there be another way? I kept coming up short during the first months. Then, in the spring, another bereaved father told me he sometimes took walks with his late daughter. He simply left the house in her company, hand in hand, and walked around the city. It seemed like a curious thing to do, but I invited Owen to come along one afternoon.

The two of us ambled across crowded sidewalks in the West Village, holding hands while talking about his field trip to the Bronx Zoo. After a few blocks, we played a game in which the first person to spot a shop we knew earned a point. When we stepped into one of them to make a purchase, Owen sat on a chair and read a book. The next day, we took another walk, this time to Chelsea. In the gift shop of a museum, Owen bought Alison a Mother's Day gift: a watch with a picture of Dali on its face. On the way home, we tried to figure out why people tend to live in neighborhoods filled with others just like them.

There were moments of plenitude on these walks, moments during which Owen's voice rose up. When we came upon a human billboard advertising a hot-dog joint, I told Owen about education and low-paying jobs, but he had a different take. "Maybe this guy likes it," he said. "Maybe he chose to do this." If I listened attentively, I could hear echoes of Owen's voice and fill in some of the holes that perforated my memory. I could also recover sides of myself that I had forgotten. Perhaps this was the way to bring him inside.

But these were mere moments. On some walks the conversation did not flow, either because I was distracted or else because Owen had nothing to say. There were even times when the two of us left the apartment together and I came home alone. Once, I answered my phone in the midst of a stroll and never went back to Owen. Another time, I asked him to sit on a bench while I made a stop at the dry cleaner's. A half hour later, far from that spot, I recalled with dismay that I had left him there. I had left Owen and never said good-bye.

Our walks became scarce by the end of the first year, but whenever I asked Owen to come along, he always put down his toys, looked up with a smile, and joined me at the door. He never complained about the time that had elapsed since our last outing. In fact, he never complained about anything, not even the life he lost at the age of eight.

Regardless, I returned to the cemetery before the first anniversary of his death and apologized to Owen. I did so twice: once for leaving him behind on the river and once for forgetting him on a bench somewhere in the big city.

NINE

*Meghan: I am sorry that Owen died and you
are probably very sad that that happened.*

fter 9/11, we spent six weeks with Owen and Julian in
a two-room hotel suite in midtown Manhattan. Battery
Park City did not feel safe, and we had not yet decided
where to go next. Though we found ourselves in close quarters, Alison and I inhabited different realms. She remained in shock; I felt confusion but no posttraumatic anxiety. I had not *lived* through the attacks, not even by watching them on TV, and this changed everything. Alison wanted me to understand what she had experienced, and continued to experience, but I had a difficult time opening myself day after day to her sorrow and uncertainty. Frightened as we both were about the future, Alison needed knowledge about potential threats whereas I sought distance. Alison also pined for reassurance, and I had none to provide, not when I stopped taking the kids on the subway because of the anthrax and the dirty bombs. Alison felt abandoned.

This is why, I later told myself, she made us vow in the tent to endure not only as a family, but also as a couple. Alison may have sensed that our responses to disaster would once again take different forms. She may have intuited that parents do not grieve in identical ways for a child who seems familiar and for a child who stands apart. And she knew that I had ended up in the water with Owen, whereas she had not. The two of us might, once again, inhabit different realms. To withstand what the future had in store, we would have to reconfigure our marriage from within.

Alison plowed through grief as if it were fresh snow. Her pain was incommensurable: she sometimes finished the day folded over on the kitchen floor, saying things like "I am cracked open" or "I am but a shell." But she also ventured into Owen's room and made regular visits to the cemetery. Several times a week, she walked along the Hudson River, all the way down to the spot in Battery Park City where she and Owen had been engulfed in white dust. I found this out three years later, when I joined her on this route for the first time. This was not her destination, she said. She simply ended up there, on a walk with Owen that had not required an invitation.

Alison ended up in other places too. One day, when taking Julian to the dentist, she found herself in the office where Owen had had his front teeth pulled weeks before the accident. She broke down in the waiting room, but this did not stop Alison. She continued to seize any opportunity to feel Owen, regardless of the potential consequences.

Alison wore Owen's watch and sometimes went to bed the way he did, staring at the wall, keeping her eyes open as long as she could, fighting slumber until, like death, it fell over her. "It's a hard way to go to sleep, but I feel like Owen," she explained.

A primal energy propelled Alison forward and thrust her into the future. She followed Owen as he grew up, imagining what he would look like at the age of nine or ten and then picturing him in his teens, his twenties, even in middle age. Every day, Alison contemplated not only what we and Owen had lost but also what we had yet to lose: an entire lineage of unborn children and grandchildren.

Unlike Alison, I kept Owen frozen in the past, with front teeth that would never come in, and reconsidered memories of an eight-year existence I had canvassed and made safe. Every intimation of Owen's life progressing, even as a figment of my imagination, was another reminder of implacable death, the end of everything.

His past did not necessarily prove more comforting. I seldom entered Owen's room, which remained as it had been before he died. In the early days, his comic books were still current, the sheets carried traces of his perspiration, the air that wafted through the window was as warm as it had been the last night he had slept there. No blown lightbulbs, no discolored posters.

Within weeks, the room became something else: a sepulcher but also a time capsule. Whenever I looked in, I thought of our apartment the day after 9/11. That morning, I had talked my way through police checkpoints and somehow made it down to Battery Park City to recover our dog, who had spent the night at home, alone. Upon walking into the apartment, I realized that the windows had been left open. A smooth blanket of dust covered every surface, creating a chillingly gorgeous fantasy of post-Vesuvius Pompeii. The entire apartment was white except for a brown circle on the bed: the dog, alive but immobile until I shook him from his torpor. Owen's room now reminded me of this scene, but without the sublime beauty or the live animal on top of the covers.

I stayed out.

I also avoided the parking lot where we had taught Owen how to ride a bike the previous summer. When friends presented us with photographs of him or poems they had written in his honor, I hid them because if I stopped to look, I would feel the promise of childhood and, again, the enormity of death— Owen's and my own. I refused to open our photo albums for similar reasons. Sometimes I told myself to plunge into the loss and touch what remained of Owen's presence. But the pain was so piercing—pain and the possibility of irreversible descent— that I mostly glanced from afar.

Outside the house, my eyes scanned the sidewalk a block ahead for parents and young children. I learned to spot them without paying attention, like a radar in default mode, and then to adjust my path or my pace to avoid overhearing fathers teach their eight-year-olds about Alexander the Great. I mention this specific example because one day I miscalculated and ended up too close.

This was a rare occurrence. In general, the mechanisms I had devised protected me from unexpected encounters. The only place in which I did not hold back was my writing. Two Word files were always open on my laptop, the day's task and my journal. Sometimes, I left the work document in the middle of a paragraph and returned after five minutes, or twenty, or perhaps not until the next day. If far from my desk, I jotted down thoughts on scraps of paper that I stuffed in my pockets.

This writing sometimes made me feel like a voyeur of our distressed lives. Private pain can all too easily become public spectacle, even if it is not shared. I could not imagine that Owen, who was secretive and did not yield to authority, would have allowed someone else to draw his portrait, even his father. Besides, how could I capture the depths of a person whom I brought

into the world but did not fully know? We raise children with
the hope or conviction that we will know them, but so much escapes us. Writing about Owen felt like an affront. Not a second
death—these words are too strong, although I heard them—but
a confiscation, a flattening. It was inadequate and unjust.

But it was less inadequate, less unjust than silence. So I kept
writing.

I wrote in expiation, in homage, in remembrance. Perhaps
someone will one day collect the scattered remains of this child's
life. Maybe it will be Julian once he grows up, or one of Owen's
friends, or a stranger who, after hearing about a boy from New
York who drowned in the Green River, will wonder what this
was all about, why did he die, what does it mean that he died,
and also who was this boy, what life did he live. This may happen, but I could not be sure, so it was up to me to gather the
vestiges of this life and death.

I wrote so that Owen would know that I had tried to understand. I wrote so that Owen would not be alone. Alison thought
it might be the other way around. Perhaps I wrote to feel less
alone, she said.

I wrote to find out if I still existed, to make sure I had not
vanished on the river. I wrote to stop roaming the streets. I wrote
because otherwise I would have had to live all of the time.

I wrote for Alison and Julian—to leave traces of Alison and
Julian, to leave traces for Alison and Julian. But, as I did so, I also
felt myself retreating from the world and the ones I loved. Writing and everyday life became distinct realms between which I
circulated without fully existing in either one. The psychiatrist
Elisabeth Kübler-Ross urged parents who have lost a child to
steer clear of Valium. She did not issue the same warning about
writing. I do not think that many mental health professionals
do: writing is deemed therapeutic. Stéphane Mallarmé could

never complete his poetic *tomb* (as he called it) for his eight-year-old son, a vault that would encase "the immense void produced by what would be his *life*—because he does not *know* it—that he is dead." Still, the fragments Mallarmé wrote must have provided something, if only deeper immersion within that void. But I wondered toward the end of the first year. Writing tempers the hurt, but might it not also deaden nerve endings? Writing can prove less painful than life, but might this mediated existence not keep experience at a remove?

Alison's walks and my writing helped us both function. We got up and showered every morning. We went out with friends. We attended weekly meetings with a therapist who specialized in grief and trauma. Though Alison had to sit still and I could not write, we both looked forward to sessions that, unlike the usual couples therapy, were meant to anticipate and prevent marital discord, to detect shifts in our dynamic in real time.

The two of us had low days during which we could not be sure we still belonged among the living, but oddly enough we did not have these days at the same time. It is as if each one of us carried a thermometer that measured the other's emotional temperature. Whoever had the lowest reading instinctively understood his or her obligation toward the other. There were things that could not be said on those days. Here we were in sync.

We also entertained equally conflicted relationships to work, which we resumed a month or so after the accident. I plugged away at my research because I had to plug away at something, but without any sense of necessity or a grasp of the larger stakes or even the pleasure I used to feel while combing through archives. I became a historian pro forma, absent from professional meetings, unable to comprehend common phrases in my field, such as "the crisis of late modernism." What could this mean? Why would people write such things?

Alison told me not to give up, perhaps because she feared that, if I did, she might give up herself. But even in the classroom, which I used to approach like a seasoned performer, capable of owning the stage or improvising with my students, I now rarely ventured beyond the lectern, rarely made any point with conviction. Grief such as ours may have cognitive consequences: for several years, I struggled to remember the names of students. But it went beyond this: I suffered from a crisis of audacity and authority, rooted in my inability to know anything for certain.

Alison's difficulties were of a different order. As a family mediator, she helped people resolve conflicts, improve relationships, and work through separations, divorces, or custody battles with as little acrimony as possible. The tenets of the profession forbid mediators from proposing solutions: it is all about listening to the two parties and helping them hear each other. Alison could still do this. At home, she instinctively listened to what Julian or I had to say, focusing not on the words themselves but on what lay behind them. Julian had experienced something that we struggled to understand: he had watched his only sibling, his rival for parental attention, simply vanish. When he belittled his brother, which still sometimes happened after the accident, Alison did not defend Owen. Instead, she listened. This is how we learned about Julian's competitive relationship with Owen, even in death, and his desire to maintain a truthful memory of his brother. In his eyes, the problem was not that Alison and I were talking too much about Owen. Rather, it was that we (or others) might turn him into an infallible hero. Julian cut Owen down to size to preserve his authentic self.

At work, too, Alison could still listen. She sometimes lost her train of thought but remained capable of immersing herself in the lives of others, even when the matter at hand seemed insignificant compared to the death of a child.

Alison was nonetheless reluctant to resume her career. It was due neither to apathy nor diminished abilities. If she resisted work, it was because she was afraid of leaving Owen behind. Making mediation a larger part of her daily life would curtail the space available for Owen. It would also suggest that his death had made room for other pursuits, that it had set her on a new and perhaps fulfilling course. This she could not accept.

Still, Alison and I returned to work. An out-of-town friend who was passing through New York whispered over lunch that she'd heard that we were—she searched for words here—living in a kind of wondrous state. She could not spell it out when I asked her what she meant. "Heroism, strength of some kind," she said. Her words echoed those we had read in condolence cards:

I admire your courage and your ability to forge ahead.

Just wanted to tell you (and I know it seems stupid) how much I admire your strength and your courage.

You are so brave. I wish there was no need to be but you are so very courageous.

A college friend told us we were his heroes. Another, we heard, was describing Alison as a saint. "That is how most people see us," Alison remarked. She said this with sadness because, while she could understand why people needed to portray us this way, such labels made her feel misunderstood, turned into an empty exemplar. The people who said this were close friends, too. If they no longer knew her, then who did?

Once or twice I told Alison that I should remain in bed for a week or more—as long as it took. I was beginning to think that showing up every day as if things were normal precluded true recognition of how much we had lost. To feel Owen's absence and presence, shouldn't I lie in a dark room, cut off from work and noises and the demands of the world? Alison never considered doing this; she did not like these conversations. But she did not ask me *not* to stay in bed. The only thing she said was that I was protecting myself a lot.

While I did not perceive this comment as a judgment, I could not help but compare my grief to hers. From where I stood, everything had fallen into place for her: acceptance of life's hazards, our path forward, Owen's presence, opening herself to what Julian had to say. It was as if she had been preparing for this moment her entire life. She did not need self-protection because she had nothing to fear, not even pain, since it deepened her connection to Owen.

When Alison talked about this connection, she never suggested that hers was the only path. She just wanted me to know. But she embraced it with such conviction and derived such strength from it that *connection* became a buzzword around the house. For me, it loomed as a mirage, an ideal that I should have attained but could not. Writing down memories was not enough, especially when I could not recover Owen's vulnerability, or Owen needing me. Like everything else, this came easily to Alison.

Before going to the cemetery, she would pick up one of the

heart-shaped rocks she had spotted on her walks and collected at home for this purpose. I scrounged for candy in the car or pebbles on a path. Next to her pure connections and deliberate offerings, mine seemed paltry and haphazard.

During the first months, I watched Alison with awe, unable to understand how she could be so certain during these most uncertain of times. I once asked her to explain what it meant to connect. She was reluctant to give advice, but did suggest that I open myself and let it come. I could not follow. My life was growing ever more bifurcated, between life with Owen and life without Owen, between the outside world and the written world, between opening up to our new reality and withdrawing within myself. Alison's, in contrast, struck me as incomprehensibly and sometimes unbearably whole. It was not envy I felt but sadness and shame before my inability to withstand the pain and recover Owen's presence.

One evening, Alison showed me a selfie that Owen had taken on her phone. I did not want to look, I did not think I could, but she insisted. Owen seemed surprisingly young in that picture.

"He feels so far," I said.

"He feels so close," Alison replied. I heard disappointment in her voice.

Alison was returning to the kids' school the next day with copies of the books Owen had been reading that last summer. In each one she had inserted a bookplate bearing his name. She did not expect me to accompany her, and I did not intend to. But as she packed her bag in the morning, I asked to come along. In the classroom, I listened as she told the kids that we had wanted to give them keepsakes. Some children remembered seeing Owen read these books. I was glad to witness this and grateful to Alison.

But some of the kids' facial features were maturing, and for this, for bringing me into this future, I was less thankful. At the end of the school year, I did not join Alison at the fourth grade's moving-up ceremony. That night, she told me she regretted my absence. She regretted it for me, she said, though I think she also regretted it for herself.

It was typically at night that Alison's grief spilled over. Lying in bed, she would read an entry from Owen's poetry book or ask about his piggy bank: What should we do with his money? Then she was gone, she collapsed in exhaustion, and I remained with the questions and images and silence. During the early months, I would listen to her during those late hours. But after a while I asked Alison why she had to wait until the end of the day to unload such things. She said it was easier in the dark and also that nighttime alone brought stillness.

Eventually, I told Alison that this was more than I could handle. I said this with desperation because I wanted us to grieve together and could not bear abandoning her as I had after 9/11. I told Alison that I was empty inside, but felt something deeper, as if I were leaving her at the river's edge. For this, too, I felt ashamed.

An acquaintance stopped me in the street in the early months, pursed her lips, and asked if Alison and I were still together. "So many couples split up after losing a child," she said. Someone else emailed that up to 85 percent of such couples end up divorcing. Whether such numbers were accurate or not, I was all too ready to believe them. In novels, movies, and TV shows, bereaved spouses struggle to mourn in unison. They spin off into different states and stop discussing their child.

But this is not because they no longer understand each other.

On the contrary, these spouses know each other's pain all too well. They are simply too diminished to provide what the other needs at any given moment. The bereaved parent's inner life is so tumultuous—such density of thought, so many overlapping emotions, so much to feel and observe within—that it saps energy and makes it difficult to look beyond oneself. Alison once told me she could not take care of me, that she would not know where to begin. I once sat next to her as she sobbed and only caressed her arm. It was not clear to me whether I was unable or unwilling to do more, but the thought did cross my mind that Alison might drag me down.

She must have felt the same at some point. I certainly assumed that she did. I remember reading about a bereaved mother who watched her husband break down in the cereal section of the grocery store—she was standing at the end of the aisle. She watched him cry and left him there. It was not a question of love. She stayed away because she had nothing to give him at that moment and perhaps because she was frightened. This seemed horrible when I read it, but within a few months it made perfect sense.

The novelist Philippe Forest, whose daughter died of cancer at the age of four, concluded that the bereaved parent must accept the impossibility of consoling his or her spouse. For Forest, this was where true love reached its limits, but also where it attained its purest and most paradoxical form. "To abandon the person one loves to despair—because this despair has become the essence of that person's life—can be a sign of love," he wrote. It can be, but neither Alison nor I were prepared to live or grieve apart, without Owen's other parent, without the only other person who knew Owen's life and death in such intimate detail.

I could not tell where this refusal originated. It is possible that tragedy on the edges of civilization, the profound isolation we had felt on the river, and the estrangement, the *strangeness* of what happened during the first twenty-four hours, drew us together. The pact we sealed in the tent was also a commitment to who we had been until the accident.

Alison and I kept trying. More couples therapy, more walks. We signed up for joint yoga lessons, hoping for communion through the body. But we stopped after three or four months because Alison was more limber than I was and also because yoga is ultimately about one's private world. Alison then took up crocheting—with the same compulsion that I invested in my writing. This made her sit still but also brought her deeper into herself.

A few months after the accident, a mother whom Alison had met at school told her she had communicated with Owen. This woman, who had been channeling for twenty years, said that Owen had been crying, that she consoled him, and also that an older man was watching over him. This conversation further convinced Alison that Owen's spirit was alive around her. He had more to say. She hired a medium, who reported that Owen did not want any more trees in his memory. We had planted a Japanese maple in Woodstock, and friends had dedicated a cherry tree to him in a Manhattan park. That's enough, Owen said.

This is all I knew about Alison's conversation with the medium. She would have told me more, but I did not ask and she refrained from broaching the topic. The book I was writing at that time (begun before the accident) revolved around the afterlife of Nostradamus's predictions over the centuries, but from a cultural historian's perspective. The idea had come to me after 9/11, when this astrologer's *Prophecies* climbed the bestseller lists. While I had never consulted these prophecies, I had read articles about them as a teenager and felt the power of interpretations that threatened a Soviet missile attack upon Western Europe in the early 1980s. After 9/11, I watched in awe as so many people turned to cryptic verses that had somehow survived for five centuries. Rather than redeem or debunk this phenomenon, my book would explain what such predictions had meant to men and women in the past and why they continued to resonate in our era.

But something strange happened a few months after the accident. One afternoon, the silver frame around a picture of Owen went dark for half a second. I saw no shadows in the room, no refraction of light. An odd thought crossed my mind: Could it be that, after sending signs to Alison, Owen was communicating with me as well? But what did I know about signs, and when have I ever believed in them? I could neither embrace nor shake this belief. When I began experiencing physical ailments, a voice inside my head intoned that Nostradamus was venting anger at me. This voice was not mine, and yet I could not stifle it. I told myself that these were mind games and that I did not have to play along. But on some days I ended up arguing it out against myself.

My internal battles with magical thinking made me resent Alison's certainty when it came to Owen's presence and dread her peregrinations with people who claimed to communicate with him. When she called to tell me about the channeler, I was furious about this woman's intrusion into our life. More frightening still was the possibility that she had indeed contacted him, whereas I still sought a comparable connection. My skepticism about what could not have taken place overlapped with fear regarding what might have.

Mostly, I feared losing Alison. She was already spending all of her days with Owen. In this psychic universe, she might now move closer to him and further away from me. It was impossible to stop Alison, and equally impossible to join her. When she suggested that we speak to the medium together, I told her I would not hear a thing.

By the end of the first year, Alison and I had stopped discussing signs and mediums, and other things, too. When I found her staring at the ceiling in bed in the morning, I did not always ask about her thoughts. When she heard me sigh, she did not always make sure I was okay. Alison said that we needed to talk more and display more affection and be sad together. What she did not explain was how to talk and give affection and feel sadness at the same time.

Neither one of us could find the words. Grief had led us to fashion a common vocabulary (the river and the accident, the tent, connection), but it also robbed our language of its potency. We had run out of adjectives, comparisons, and metaphors. Why tell each other once again that our entire bodies ached? That Owen did not deserve this? That our grief was like a rock thrown into a lake, disturbing all the particles? When one of us uttered such words, the other replied with something like *I know, this is impossible* or *It makes no sense* in order to shorten the exchange. Soon, neither one of us began such conversations.

The woman in the grocery store abandoned her husband because she did not have the strength to console him. She said so later. It dawned on me one day that she might have lacked the words as well.

A few years after the accident, I came across articles on bereaved parents and divorce that paint a less alarming picture than the one I had been told about early on. According to one, this rate falls between 9 and 16 percent. According to another, only half of these divorced couples deem their child's death an important factor. The truth is, there are few reliable numbers, few long-term studies resting on broad sample sizes. One of the authors I read said as much. But even if I had found reassuring statistics that first year, I doubt they would have done any good.

When I looked at Alison, I no longer saw the woman who used to love life and find joy in everyday activities. When Alison looked at me, she no longer found spontaneity or humor. We continued to live together, but we were losing parts of ourselves and discovering others that we had never known, so it was no longer clear to whom exactly we were married.

How can spouses who are turning into other versions of themselves, spouses who have lost desire for all things, continue to make a life together? A friend of mine, a psychologist, told me there is a surge of extramarital affairs among those who have lost a loved one or survived a serious illness. After encountering mortality, she said, we want to feel alive and shed our identity as mourners or patients. It is easier to do so with a person who has not shared or witnessed our ordeal. My friend called this an act of rebellion, the revenge of deserted possibilities.

Several years after the death of their daughter, Philippe Forest and his wife agreed to have affairs in order to recover love and desire, return to life, and uncover other sides of themselves. They stayed together while opening their marriage in this way, but I thought of them the day Alison asked me whether I had considered leaving her for someone else. Though she denied it, her question seemed to suggest that she had given the matter some thought. I answered that I had not contemplated leaving her, which was true, although I had dreamed of other women and the thrill of a life governed by pleasure. In one of these dreams, I cheated on Alison with Alison herself—Alison as she had been before the accident.

One afternoon that first winter, the two of us ventured into the snow-covered woods of Woodstock. We walked among the oak trees and hemlocks, our feet cracking the brittle ice crust. When we stopped moving, all was perfectly still and white. Alison and I took this as an invitation to lie on our backs and stare at the sky. The powder encased our bodies: two open-air tombs in the middle of a forest that was pure and desolate.

I cannot recall this scene without also thinking of the no-suicide pledge Alison and I made within weeks of the accident. We promised one another that, as dire as things might become, neither one of us would abandon the other and Julian. Everything was allowed except for this, even if ending one's life meant encountering Owen on the other side. I do not remember where this conversation took place, or who started it. Did we look into one another's eyes? Shake hands? End with an embrace? All I recall are the words themselves, the mutual promise that gave me such comfort when Alison seemed to be moving so much faster than me.

Strangely, Alison cannot recollect any pledge. In her mind, there is no such thing. It might be amnesia on her part, or involuntary fabrication on mine. Regardless, the two of us have carried our own memories, not only of Owen, but also of the grief that drew us together and apart at the same time.

TEN

Blake: *Overall, was Owen the best*
at the PlayStation game?

When evenings came, the three of us hovered around the dining room table, eyeing the empty chairs. We had not always sat in the same places, so it was not that we feared filling Owen's spot. But four has a symmetry that three does not. We could huddle together at the end of the table. We could also sit across from one another. But who, then, would sit alone? Unable to settle or even discuss the matter, we kept changing places, from one hard-edged triangle to another. Family snapshots from that time likewise display permutations of two rather than portraits of three, as if we refused to immortalize Owen's absence.

Most of these photographs include Julian, with Alison or me by his side. He was the constant presence, the boy who had lost his sibling and continued to require parenting. Julian became the center of our family life—not the sole focus, but the most urgent one. He was in seventh grade, about to morph into a teen. The years ahead would be complicated; Alison and I would have to remain attentive. I thought of it as a six-year project that would end with his departure for college. Afterward Alison and

I would hover around the dining room table on our own, imagining what it meant to become a household of two.

So many people asked us how Julian was faring. "Thank God for him," some of them said. "For his sake, you'll hold it together." Once the school year began, Alison and I made sure he arrived on time in the morning. Conferring with his teachers, we devised contingency plans in case he broke down in the middle of the day. We found a therapist in the neighborhood and bought Julian chocolate pastries after his sessions. We urged him to write down his thoughts, but did not insist when he abandoned his journal. A few months after the accident, we began planning his bar mitzvah.

We did all of this but still could not tell Julian where to sit at the dinner table. It was not the only thing that lay beyond us. We wondered what Julian understood about his own loss, how much he wanted and needed to know, and even whether part of him resented a brother who, in death as in life, took up so much of his parents' emotional lives. Though much of our grief was grounded in the micro-present—one hour, one day—we projected ourselves into the future when it came to Julian. We pondered how Owen's death would continue to take on new shapes as he moved toward his twenties, graduated from college, carved out his place in the world. How would it reroute his life and shape the things he would and would not do, his relationships, the way he raised his children?

I thought of Julian while reading a memoir whose author had stopped making friends after losing his twin brother at age six. He feared that his late brother would grow jealous of new friends. Would Julian do the same? Would he recover, at age thirty or fifty, memories of Owen and their times together? Would he feel that he had had a true childhood? Would he deem it his duty to live for two, fulfilling the aspirations Alison and I had entertained for both of our children?

Gauging Julian's current emotional state proved as difficult as imagining his future. Now and then, Julian spoke about the changes in our lives. We would never again appreciate the beauty of canyons, he remarked at one point. For Alison's birthday, he wrote a poem about missing Owen on this "awful sad" day and yet somehow celebrating his mother, who belonged to the three of us alone—Owen, myself, and Julian. In his eyes, we remained a family of four.

Julian also told us he sometimes felt he should be missing Owen more than he did. Alison thought about Owen every minute of every day (he once heard her say this), so why did he only do so three times a week?

Such revelations were rare. For the most part, Julian refrained from putting words to what he felt. He remained quiet when, in futile attempts to determine where he stood or ease what we took to be his pain, Alison and I engaged him by saying things like *I'm sorry you lost your best friend.* We were both convinced that opening up to us would make him feel less alone while helping us parent. But we could not force it. The only thing to do was to observe Julian intently. The anecdotes I transcribed in my journal also represented a desperate attempt to elucidate my child's grief, intertwined with mine and yet subject to its own unseen laws.

Some of the things we observed suggested that Julian was finding his way. He eagerly went to school in the morning, completed all of his homework assignments, and did well in the middle school geography bee. But he resented the boy who had joined Owen's class in September. *Owen's replacement*, he called him. We also found out that he commonly left class before the end; took long breaks in the school library; and was thrown off by bee questions about Utah and a town in Indiana called Owensburg.

His Little League career provided yet starker signs. Julian and Owen had shared a passion for baseball. Owen was a Yankees fan whereas Julian had for some reason chosen the Phillies. The two of them would exchange baseball cards and spend weekend mornings at Greenwich Village Little League. The first spring after the accident, Julian and I joined hundreds of kids and parents at Pier 40, where Houston meets the Hudson, for the opening day ceremony. I hung around Julian's team for a while and then walked over to Owen's just as the league director declared over the loudspeaker that the entire season would be dedicated to him. The kids did not know what to say when I showed up, but all wore jerseys with the words "Owen's Stars." The coaches had also handed out patches bearing Owen's name. Julian took one, but later confessed that he had not heard the director's remarks. He just wanted to play.

The season proved brutal. The previous spring, Julian had won a team award for his .433 batting average. Now, he found himself unable to make contact. Having lost his abilities at the plate, he would routinely slump back to the dugout after four or five pitches. On more than one occasion, he sat down after his second or third strikeout of the game and buried his face in his hands. Every at-bat became an ordeal, something that he dreaded, a failure waiting to happen.

These at-bats seemed to condense our current lives on a stage that was at once smaller and larger. Hitting a fast-moving ball with a bat that is not much wider while players and spectators stare in silence requires concentration, the ability to tune out the outside world. Julian was struggling with both—focus and the gaze of others—on a field where he probably felt Owen's absence more intensely than elsewhere. It was painful for Alison and me to watch from the stands as Julian stood at the plate, so much more exposed than we ever had to be at that time. My mother-in-law said this was the one place where she saw the emotional toll of everything Julian was living through.

Julian later wrote a high school paper about his Little League falloff. "My elaborate pre-swing routine no longer intimidated the pitcher," he wrote. "It just made him impatient." As it was happening, though, Julian never connected baseball to his life beyond the field. This left me wondering what he made of his sudden drop in performance. The answer came after the final game, when he received the dreaded sportsmanship award and then quit baseball for good. When he most needed what baseball had to offer, Julian wrote in his paper, he "felt more alone than ever."

Julian did not talk much about solitude that first year. Before the accident, he had often acted as an older brother and commanded Owen when they played together. But Owen was a natural leader, a forceful presence with deep reserves of social energy. Sometimes he would play with Julian's friends after Julian had retired to his room with a book. Around the dinner table, Owen often drew most of the attention, allowing Julian to recede into the background. Now, Julian had to finish his own playdates and fill this silence on his own.

Alison and I struggled to determine what this took out of

him though we did see him search, like an archaeologist, for traces of Owen's presence. Three months after the accident, Julian called me into his bedroom and held Owen's Little League cap to my nose. "If you breathe in hard enough," he said, "you can still smell him." He then took me to Owen's room, pointed to his erasable board, and explained that he had made out a few words in Owen's handwriting. Here was *Owen* in one corner, *suck* or something like it in another.

These connections proved fleeting, which is why when Julian wanted to hear Owen's voice, he loaded old videos on his computer, and when he wanted to bring him into the present, he played video games with his brother, filling him in on news events, such as the death of Michael Jackson nearly a year after Owen's own. When Julian wanted to see two brothers fight mercilessly until a hard-won reconciliation, he watched *Step Brothers*. He told us this was the last movie he had seen with Owen—in Utah, just days before the accident—and also the last movie Owen ever saw.

And when Julian wanted to visit Owen, he went, of all places, to the virtual farm on which he planted crops, plowed fields, and raised livestock. One evening, he sat me behind his laptop for an impromptu tour of his Farmville property. He pointed to the barn and stables, the cows and horses, the pastures and carrot beds. The visit ended with a pond and, next to it, a white tombstone. "This is Owen's grave, a quiet place," Julian said. Because Julian would not enter the Woodstock cemetery, I had believed that he never visited Owen's grave. In fact, he had built his own.

These glimpses into Julian's interior life suggested that he grieved with an intensity that was his alone. He was following a route that lay within his reach—and also beyond mine. Unlike him, I did not tap my senses or watch videos to feel Owen's presence. I also stayed away from the Catskills slopes on which I had taught the boys to ski. I did not think I could withstand their mix of natural beauty, physical risk, and familial intimacy. But Julian insisted that we return together. It would be hard at any time, he said, so we might as well go now.

Julian and I also entertained different relationships to the scene of the accident. Though he sometimes claimed to block it out, he announced one evening that he had located the rapids on Google Maps. There they were on his laptop, a crisp photograph that he blew up until he and I stood so close to the water that my body trembled. Julian saw me turn away from the screen. In my mind, this meant that he grasped what I had been sensing for months but struggled to acknowledge: how much I now fell short as his father.

An acquaintance had emailed me that, ever since the death of her teenage sister two decades earlier, she had felt that her parents "were somehow hating me for what happened (rather than loving me even more)." I do not think that this applied to us; I do not think that we blamed or repudiated or neglected Julian, whether out of anger or despair. But Alison once told me she was not parenting Julian well, and I felt equally diminished. Even as friends wrote us that Owen's death inspired them to become more attentive parents, I grew increasingly aware of what I could not provide.

When one of my nephews, four at the time, sang to Julian that his brother was dead, I did not know what to say, and thus said nothing. When Julian broke down at the sight of a dead toad by the road—the kind of toad he and Owen used to seek out in Woodstock—I looked on in a stupor, unable to understand that when Julian said, *It was alive just a moment ago, I was holding it yesterday, and now it is dead,* he was grappling with Owen's death. Several months had passed since the accident, and yet this still escaped me.

I declined Julian's invitation to watch the Major League Home Run Derby because it was something I had done with Owen two weeks before his death and the memory remained too raw, and also because of the many other things I could not do, the most grueling was to take Owen's place.

Sometimes Julian wanted me closer and sometimes, like all teenagers, he pushed me away. After our pact in the tent, I could not imagine how any one of us could venture alone into the world. I kissed Julian repeatedly, touched him as he walked by, and held him tight in embraces he had to break. One morning, I asked him if we could hold hands on the way to school. He refused at first before relenting, but only for a block. Though Julian rarely saw me cry after the first weeks, he heard me sigh throughout the day and also report on my state of mind, dark though it may have been.

With Owen gone, Julian had to combine his own temperament with Owen's to serve as confidant and accomplice, partner in jokes and political conversations. I could not stop teaching him: advice, admonitions, warnings, life lessons. The chain of transmission now ended with Julian: everything I had to impart, anything I might hope to bequeath, would now pass through him alone. I knew that it was too much, that no child can meet all these parental expectations, but I could not stop.

I also knew how much Julian needed space to fall and fail and hurt himself, to grapple with his own fears, but here too, I found it impossible to step back. Julian balked the day I forbade him to climb a rooftop water tower pylon. For a while, I believed that I was responding to what I had learned about the hazards of the world. I enforced rules and boundaries to prepare him for what might await. Only later did I realize that this was less about Julian than about me as a father. I could not lapse, I could not let him go.

Julian also told me I was too strict, too serious. "You don't laugh anymore," he said. "I am the only one who laughs in this family." This was true. Julian's raucous laughter had returned, whereas I no longer made practical jokes or teased people whom I loved. So much of my relationship with Owen and Julian had revolved around play, but now the sense of play, the *possibility* of play and everything it suggested about innocence and lightness of being, had become incomprehensible. Laughter and play felt like a tacit betrayal of Owen, as if play and pain could not coexist.

At the end of Julian's school year, I invited him to call in sick one morning and play hooky with me. We took the subway to Astoria, Queens, where we ate breakfast in a Greek deli, got haircuts from an Uzbek barber, and walked around a neighborhood that neither one of us knew. This discovery, this break from routine, this contempt for rules felt sweet and forbidden. It also felt poignant, at least to me, since Owen and I had often talked about one day skipping school and work and eating pizza all day in front of the TV. Much as I relished the time with Julian, I am not certain I laughed that day in Queens.

Soon after the accident, an old friend invited me to "find the courage to teach Julian to become a happy man." Her words stayed with me: a worthy, necessary endeavor. But they required a belief in the possibility of happiness as well as an almost child-like trust in the world and humankind and the future. This called for more strength than I could muster on most days. Regardless, when another friend asked at the end of the first year for the deepest insight I had gained since the accident, I quoted this line. This friend replied that it might also work the other way. "Maybe," he said, "Julian heard somewhere that he needs the courage to teach his father to become a happy man."

I cannot imagine that Julian deemed his efforts successful. In time, he complained about my unwelcome hugs, my emotional needs, and my inability to let him act his age. If the two of us were movies, he said, he would be *Step Brothers* and I would be *Shoah* (he had somehow heard about the classic Holocaust documentary). There were times when Julian berated me mercilessly, pushing the limits of acceptable language in public put-downs. This began soon after the accident, a reflection of his anger and loneliness, which pushed him to seek out immediate responses. Beyond the usual teen behavior, he was probably also testing me, making sure I could still stand tall. I sometimes wondered why Julian did not treat his shrunken father with more compassion, but could not let such thoughts distract from the task at hand: respond to Julian in a measured way, neither too meek nor too rough.

He must have felt my confusion, my sense that nothing was assured anymore—certainly not my authority as a parent. After the accident, what degree of confidence could I retain in this domain or any other? My sense of self was so compromised that, while I continued to advise and admonish Julian, I did so without being convinced that I was correct. There were times when I backed off in his presence, and times when I stood my ground with an obstinacy that belied my doubts. I hoped Julian would tell me many years hence that, after the accident, I had done the best I could under the circumstances. I could not be sure this would happen, which is why, I suspect, I left a written record of myself as a father—diminished, uncertain, but present.

Alison, too, buzzed around Julian. We both did, seeking the same attention and affection as parents, and sometimes we collided. Alison had long been the primary caregiver, but now one of her sons was gone, the other thinking about high school, and her husband spent more time at home. I wish that I had asked her how this felt, but I was too busy staking out a new position. When Julian tested me, Alison told me to just go with it. She also said I was too demanding of him. More than boundaries, he needed love and levity and the right to remain a child. This is what she sought to provide.

She did not doubt her ability to do so because her sense of self and her authority as a parent remained intact. I made sense of this by returning to the fact that Alison had not been in the ducky with Owen. It is also possible, however, that our culture still conditions men more than women to experience a violent loss such as ours as a lack of competence, a failure on the job. Our couples therapist threw out this idea, and I found it compelling. When my eldest son seemed to turn against me and my wife urged me to do better, I liked to think that deeper social forces were also at play. In the same situation, other fathers might have responded in ways not unlike mine.

A year after the accident, Alison's mother invited Julian to pick a photograph from her collection as a bar mitzvah gift. She is a photographer and collector whose fine eye enabled her to make smart acquisitions in the 1970s, before prices began to soar. Julian chose Diane Arbus's *A Family on Their Lawn One Sunday in Westchester, N.Y.* and hung it above his bed.

A few years later, a friend noticed the photograph. "What an incredibly depressing picture," she said, and asked me for the backstory. Her instinctive response was that it must have expressed what Julian felt at the time. Until that moment, I had never considered this photograph as a scan of Julian's psyche. Nor had Alison. We had looked the other way or else missed what now seemed so obvious besides suburban anomie or inattentive parenting: a family of three, together and yet separate within an empty expanse.

The thing is, I still do not know what Julian found so alluring. At first, I was convinced that it was the photograph's bleakness. No one laughs in this family. Lying side by side, the parents are secluded in their respective universes. The father, unable to look up, purses his lips in what may well be a sigh, similar to my own sighs, which Julian monitored with unremitting vigilance.

Julian would comment during that first year about the gray that bled across my beard and the wrinkles at the corners of Alison's eyes, all of these signs of depletion and aging that made him anxious. If we died, Julian would be left alone, like the boy in the background, out of his parents' sight, eager to play but on his own.

This may be what Julian saw in the photograph. But it is also true that, while the parents remain immobile—whether checked out or exhausted or overwhelmed, they are clearly stuck in place—the boy is caught in motion. I initially thought he was struggling to set up his miniature pool, but then I pictured a scene in which he prepared to fill it with water so that his parents could refresh themselves on that summer day. Looking at the photograph, Julian may have seen a boy who, though he wanted to play, also nurtured his parents.

That is after all what he had done following Owen's death. He glanced at Alison during movie scenes that involved mothers and sons. Once, after Alison told him that having him nearby made her less sad, he replied that, for her sake, he had better not die anytime soon. She needed him too much. Without Julian, I would not have returned to the ski slopes, or smelled Owen's baseball cap, or, after doing so and waiting for Julian to fall asleep that night, entered Owen's room for the first time in months, sat on his bed, stared at undiscernible words on his erasable board, and felt a sliver of his presence.

Arbus may not have depicted a harmonious or functional family, but she did place a family at the center of her composition. Our own familial disorder unsettled Julian so much that he objected whenever one of us declared that we had become a different family. We are the same, he insisted. To make certain, he kept telling us that he remained a kid. The desperation in his voice telegraphed his need for clear boundaries as well as his inability to serve as a makeshift parent all of the time. If I resumed my role as a father, then he could return to his as a child.

I sometimes wondered for whom things are in the end more difficult: the parents of a bereaved child or the child whose parents mourn his lost brother. Both losses are of course painful in their own ways, but I kept returning to the question, perhaps because I still knew so little about Julian's inner life. Family tragedies can sharpen the senses and open the heart, but they do not necessarily allow parents to better understand their children. The novelist Annie Ernaux, whose sister died at the age of six, may have said it best: "The parents of a deceased child do not know what their pain does to the child who remains." All they can do is imagine what it might feel like to suffer losses so different from their own: the sibling who has died and the parents who now seem adrift.

ELEVEN

Fiona: *How did you find out he died?*

Everything changed the moment we recovered Owen's body. An hour or more after the accident, one of the guides carried a ducky upstream and retraced the route we had taken through the rapids. Soon afterward, a three-person party crossed the river to search for Owen on the other bank. Its leader was Kris, the thirtysomething guide who had given the safety briefing that morning and then piloted the raft in which Owen and I had ridden until lunch. He had manned the oars and told stories about the dinosaurs that once inhabited the area. He also told us he had run rivers for years, working hard during the summer and decamping abroad with Delma in the winter. South America was next.

I remember Kris as tall and rugged and lanky, with a pointy nose and a ponytail. Delma had dirty blond hair, a tanned, freckled face, and a stout body. The two of them embodied American archetypes—the trapper and the beach bum—that I had encountered in movies and TV shows while growing up in Brussels. Which is to say that, from my perspective, we had little in common. They moved with agility in this lunar landscape and could talk about rock formations and geological time. I imagined that, after the summer, they returned to a nomadic life in natural expanses that spoke to them in ways people like me could not. In truth, I had no idea what the two of them thought or how they lived their lives.

The second member of the search party was another vacationer, a fit, middle-aged man from San Francisco who was traveling with a friend. I know nothing else about him, not even his name.

I was the third member of the party. For a long time, I was convinced that Delma had asked me to join them because she knew that something momentous lay ahead and sensed that the father whose son was missing should be present. But years after the accident I spoke to Alison about this and realized that I had insisted upon going along. As time ticked away, as the guides moved with growing urgency, as the vacationers continued to search for a child they had hardly met in a place they did not know while beginning to consider, as they must have, that things might not end well, I had told Delma I would make the crossing.

Kris maneuvered the raft across the river without our help. We disembarked and scrambled upstream, climbing where necessary, keeping our eyes on the ground. Kris went first, looking up the hills, searching for Owen behind boulders. I followed, examining the same places but with less confidence that we would find him on land. Couldn't Owen have been pinned under a rock in the water? Unlikely, Kris said. So voluble that morning, he now kept quiet except for warnings about loose stones. The traveler from San Francisco followed without saying a word. I heard the crackling of our shoes on the dirt and the lapping of the river a few feet away.

At one point, Kris walked ahead and vanished from view. The other traveler and I continued on our own for a few minutes, until a guide appeared around a bend. I think it was Kris though I am not certain; by that time, other guides may have crossed the river as well. My inability to remember unnerves me. What kind of witness am I bearing if I cannot describe these events with precision?

The guide said that Owen had been found underwater. Your son is dead, he said.

This I remember clearly—and also having to catch my breath.

I crouched on the rocky earth and looked at Owen's body through the brush and low trees. He lay on a slightly elevated plateau two hundred feet away, his legs stretched out on the hot rock. Kneeling by his side, the guide who had gone upstream was giving him mouth-to-mouth resuscitation. Owen had been growing that year, his limbs lengthening, his stomach bulging a little, his cheekbones protruding. But from where I was he seemed small. His white T-shirt made his body seem so bright that it almost sparkled against the vast landscape.

I saw Owen but also myself, as if I had slipped out of my skin and took in the scene at a distance. Shot from above, the frame included the boy's body, the guide hunched above, the father crouching behind brush, a man in wet clothes standing a few feet behind, and water flushing down the canyon. Books on grief advise mourners to take a good look at the body of the deceased, but I did not move.

———

Why am I not rushing over to Owen? Why am I not holding his body, checking his pulse, kissing his cheeks? Why am I still crouching behind the brush?

That evening, I told Alison that Owen had looked peaceful. His skin was smooth, without gashes or bruises or bloating. When Alison asked again months later, I added that his eyes were shut and his hair neatly arranged. His face seemed calm, without a trace of anguish. This is what I saw from where I was, I told her.

At some point, Delma appeared on the other bank and gestured instructions. Someone said we should get going. I took a last look, stood up, and turned around. The traveler from San Francisco walked ahead. After witnessing this unthinkable moment in my life—the life of a stranger—he now had to escort me back to the raft. A death walk with a bereaved father: somehow, there was space in my brain to consider what was expected of him.

Kris must have been with us as well, although he and I never spoke again. He did not say anything during that walk, or that night in camp, or the next morning on the way to Echo Park, or after the guides broke their embrace by the river. Each time his face pops up in my mind—a regular occurrence during the first year, less so now—his features harden a little. I still do not know if it is shock I saw in his eyes that day, or contrition, or even anger.

Nor do I know what he saw in mine beyond shock. For a long time, I believed that he did not see anger. But when I first began writing about the river, I omitted Kris's name and referred to him only as Ponytail.

———

As we neared the raft, I saw people setting up camp on the other side of the river. Word must have gone out that we would spend the night on that narrow beach because tents were going up. Alison was now standing by the water. Once we began the crossing and her face came into focus, it became obvious that she knew. She later told me that one of the guides had walked up to Julian and her minutes earlier, as they drove tent stakes into the ground, and murmured that Owen had been found. Soon afterward, Julian went into the tent to cry on his own.

Once we were close enough, I jumped over the side of the raft and ran toward Alison. We held one another without speaking, hands gripping shoulders with the force of the hugs we would give Owen before he went to sleep. He always requested tight embraces that squeezed his rib cage and took his breath away.

I wish I could convey with befitting eloquence what a parent feels upon learning that his child has died in such circumstances. All I know is what did not happen.

I did not feel vital energy seep out of me.

I did not buckle or collapse, flattened on the dirt.

I did not sweat or shiver.

I did not gasp or put my hands to my face.

I did not look up to the sky or stare down toward the ground.

The light did not grow dim; the air did not dry up. If I uttered any words, I do not recall what they were.

So it is not true that *everything* changed the moment we recovered Owen's body.

When Odysseus's mother believed that her son had died, she pined for him day and night, weeping until death befell her. "Not that illness overtook me—no true illness wasting the body," her spirit later told Odysseus. "Only my loneliness for you . . . took my own life away."

When Victor Hugo found out that his daughter Léopoldine had perished, he nearly went mad. "For three days I wept bitterly! I wanted to gash my head against the ground," he wrote in a poem he entitled "At First, Oh! I Was Like a Maniac."

When Isadora Duncan learned that her two children had drowned in the Seine (her driver had stepped out of their car without putting on the brakes), she collapsed and then, that night, kneeled to watch over the two bodies until morning. A witness declared: "The grieving mother, eternally frozen in sorrow, remains cloistered in her room."

When Alison learned that Owen had drowned in a river, she did not weep until death befell her. She did not gash her head against the ground. Nor did she collapse or cloister herself. Alison set up a tent and held me tightly, body upright, feet planted in the sandy earth.

TWELVE

Delia: *I feel sad about Owen's death
and I feel bad for you.*

Owen died and all of our parents, Alison's and mine,
had to cope with the loss of their grandson. They had
to mourn Owen while measuring the impact of his
death on their own children as well as Julian. During the early
weeks in Woodstock, they cleaned the house and prepared meals
and welcomed visitors. It sometimes felt as if Alison and I became children again, under the care of relatives who shielded us
as best they could from their own pain.

But the two of us also took on the parental role. The death
of a child upends the filial relationship as much as others. When
our parents grow old, we observe them with care while antici-
pating our own dotage. What, however, could they teach Alison
and me in this situation? There were no previous experiences
from which they might draw, nothing to serve as a road map.
Alison and I had to lead the way across a terrain that was as
mystifying to them as to us.

Our parents remained in Woodstock for a few weeks and
then left. Back in Brussels, my mother kissed Owen's photograph
every evening and occasionally ate lunch in a pizza joint he had
liked. On a corkboard in his home office, my father pinned a

note that Owen had given him a year earlier. Alison's mother assembled photos into a small shrine in her home. Her father emailed us memories of Owen whenever they surfaced. Such snippets were all I knew about their grief, which was interlaced with ours and yet remote. Their ache was palpable, but I lacked the emotional force, the will, the curiosity to ask them how they felt on any given day.

My mother longed for intimacy around Owen and our common loss. In Woodstock, she once walked from the house to my studio, softly knocked, and just stood there when I opened the door, speechless, offering me her sorrow, waiting for me to clutch her. During those early days, she talked about moving from Brussels to New York to be close to us. I could not clutch her, I could not invite her to join us in the States. I could not bear her pain and did not believe that she could shoulder mine.

At some point, my mother tried to explain what she had felt when I had called from Utah the day after the accident. *You told me to put your father on the line. I asked if everything was okay, but you didn't answer, you simply told me again to put him on the line. Right then, I knew.* As she paused to choose her words, I played out what would follow. She would tell me that she had heard me cry for the first time in years, that she had booked plane tickets in a daze, what she and my father had said to one another (or perhaps what they could not say), at what time they finally fell asleep that night (or perhaps that they never did), and also what they had felt the next morning as they left the apartment for the airport and slowly processed the fact that their son had lost his own son on a river whose name meant nothing to them. I knew what was coming, so I changed the subject. My mother slipped in another sentence—*You don't know how many times I have relived that call*—and then I shut her down. Her sorrow was hers, not mine. It was not the same.

Unlike my mother, my father kept his emotions to himself. I had only seen him cry once, decades earlier when his own father died. This made an impression because I knew so little about his inner life. My mother would take it upon herself to tell my sister and me how much he loved us, how proud he was of our accomplishments, how touched he was when we remembered his birthday. She never explained why my father could not say such things, and I never asked her, not even in my teens, when this began to strike me as a serious limitation. Looking at old birthday cards, I wondered why, under the generic copy, he would write only, *Love, Daddy*.

After Owen's death, my father cried at the funeral, in our house, and during the service on the last night of shivah. During those early days, I invited him to join me on runs to the dump just outside Woodstock. The two of us loaded empty cans and bottles in the trunk and drove to the transfer station. During one ride, I told him that he and my mother could not move to New York, that we should avoid further disruptions in our lives. Most of the time, we talked about mundane matters, which was fine. What we said mattered less than the outing itself.

As a child, I had cherished my father's affectionate embraces and boisterous stories. I loved our weekly tennis game and Saturday mornings in his corporate office, when my sister (two years younger) and I sat behind his desk and listened with pride as colleagues and underlings greeted him in reverential tones.

But the rhythms of our family life fluctuated along with his moods. His temper erupted at a moment's notice. When things did not go his way, when his authority was contested, or, quite simply, when he lost patience, he exploded, filling the house with dictates, shouts, and insults I had not even heard at school. There was physical violence, too: shoving, grabbing, kicking, occasional beltings. This violence fell upon the children alone. My mother did not know how to protect her children and could not herself escape the verbal abuse. My father's mix of tenderness and combustibility created an unstable domestic universe in which everyday life could take a frightening turn without notice. Soon enough, things returned to the way they had been—embraces, stories, visits to the office—except that memories lingered, and so did the knowledge that the cycle was bound to resume.

At the age of twelve, I stopped calling my father Daddy, opting instead for Berl, the Yiddish name that his parents used. He did not object, nor did he ask why. From then on, he signed his cards, *Love, Berl.*

The new name stuck—I never called him Daddy again, or even Dad—but it did little against his anger. In my early teens, I did forestall one of his fits of rage by asking him to tell me *why* he was so angry. This altered the dynamic, but only for a few seconds; the moment at which he stammered words of explanation was also the moment at which he realized that he had been duped. There was little hope of understanding his abrupt shifts in mood or my own conflicting feelings toward a man I wanted to love even if I never felt safe in his house.

A few years later, I left home for college in the United States. With an ocean between us, my father's demeanor softened. He sent me letters ending with "big hugs and kisses" and asked me to write back because, he said, he liked to hear from me. The summer after freshman year—which I spent in Brussels—he allowed me to stay home and work on a novel instead of finding a job.

In his late fifties by then, Berl's career ended with an unsolicited transfer to Texas—not a demotion, but a loss of status. He enrolled in a continuing education program and sent me descriptions of his courses. Regarding one, on the interpretation of dreams, he wrote, "What if I prefer not to know the meaning of my dreams?" Around that time, he came down with symptoms that doctors could not diagnose: vertigo, weakness in his limbs, lack of energy. Sometimes panic seized him—panic fueled by a fear of dying. "Hold me," I once heard him implore my mother.

The symptoms eventually passed, and then Berl retired and moved back to Brussels, where he taught accounting at a local college. Throughout my twenties, I resisted confronting the darker sides of his personality. I sent him Father's Day cards in which I described him as loving and supportive, an irreplaceable parent and friend. After I embarked on a career as a historian, the two of us would chat about the modern university or European unification. When my first book won accolades, he wrote to congratulate me: "Although you were never interested in commerce, your ability to conceive an idea and follow its implementation is a quality that I sought when hiring people in business." This was a high compliment. Though he couched it in the jargon of his profession, he was trying to understand my life on its own terms. So it felt to me.

I sometimes tried to understand him as well. In his home office, my father had hung a photograph of himself and his brother as children, seated around their parents on a sofa. It is a warm scene, the two boys lounging and smiling, Berl's brother and mother wrapped in one another's arms. But his father sits stiffly in a dark suit, staring at the camera with a closed face and his hands on his lap. Berl is alone to his right, arms crossed and eyes darting toward the center. Looking at this picture, I could feel affection for a boy whose father may have imposed his own severe discipline at home.

My empathy only went so far, however. Though Berl was no longer physically violent, I retained a muscle memory of his abuse. I remained on guard in his presence, recoiling if he made a sudden motion too close to me.

I never figured out what he made of my diffidence. During one of my visits to Brussels, he invited me to accompany him to a reception with some of the professors he had befriended. I said yes, then changed my mind, invoking jet lag. The truth was, I did not want to be alone with him in the car and then pretend to be his academic colleague while feeling compelled to make him proud. Berl stood awkwardly in the living room for long seconds, playing with his keys, giving me an opportunity to change my mind without asking me to do so. Then he left and never brought the matter up again.

There was something unexpected, then, about asking my father to drive with me to the dump. He may have felt this, too. "I'm not good at showing emotions," he told me after the accident, "but I'm here." He now deferred to me, out of respect—as I saw it—for an experience he could not fathom. I do not remember him raising his voice in my presence that first year. He grew concerned when, during my first visit to Brussels, I went out one evening and forgot to call by our agreed-upon time. The next day, he came looking for me in the bathroom because I had been there longer than usual.

All of this was touching, but disorienting as well. While I cautiously let Berl in during those months, I resented his inability to provide a home in which I could have learned to trust my instincts, assert myself, and say no when necessary. The thought now went through my head that, had he done so, I might have made different decisions on the river.

Berl soon avoided all talk about Owen and life without

Owen—as if he once again preferred not to know. He asked my mother not to kiss Owen's photograph in his presence and, shortly afterward, forbade her from uttering his name when he was in the room. While he never made such demands of me, he remained quiet whenever I mentioned Owen. He never shared memories or expressed regret or voiced wistfulness. On the first anniversary of the accident, he neither called nor emailed.

I told myself that his pain remained so intense and frightening that he had to lock Owen away in order to contain it, that his behavior was not so different from my own inability to look at photo albums. Still, all I now encountered in his presence was silence—a silence that seemed to erase my child's existence.

There were times when this silence was my own, when I kept quiet or stayed away from my father. Owen was not only my son, but also his grandson. I felt responsible for his sorrow (and my mother's as well), ashamed even. I had invested so much emotional energy in becoming a good father—a father who was present and self-critical and spurned physical violence. The shame I now felt as both a son and a father made it difficult to spend long stretches with Berl. It drove us further apart.

A few years before the accident, my parents offered to keep Owen and Julian at their Brussels home while Alison and I spent a weekend in the country. After loading up the car, I took my father aside in the kitchen and asked him to control his temper in the children's presence. It was not an easy thing to say and, as quickly became apparent, not an easy one for him to hear. It all came back: the anger taking hold of him, his body encroaching upon mine, the booming voice that filled the room, the spittle and narrowed eyes. This time, however, I leaned against a cabinet for support and told my father as steadily as I could that this was the way it had to be with my children. He stared at me and then slowly walked away, wiping his mouth with his handkerchief. My heart was pounding, but at that moment I felt like the better father.

After Owen died, the benchmark for a good father was revealed to be stark: keep your children physically safe, carry them into adulthood. This is how I now saw it—a simple matter. Berl had succeeded and I had not, which is why I could no longer imagine surpassing him as a father. Regardless of what he might say, regardless of what he might shout, the very sight of my father now reminded me of what else I had lost on the river.

THIRTEEN

Claire: *How long can you go without
thinking about him?*

G rief is surrounded by expectations. When people whispered my name or gently touched my shoulder, I made eye contact, bit my lower lip, and nodded once or twice. We did not have to speak to play our respective roles: the empathetic acquaintance and the bereaved father. When people inquired whether Alison and I talked about Owen every single day, I listened to my answer in the hope of learning something. But when they asked how we were carrying on, I squirmed. If I told them that I still felt hollow, they might recoil in fear. If I said I was all right, they might conclude that I was papering over my innermost feelings or, worse still, expressing what I really felt.

There were other impossible moments. On my first visit to the High Line, the public park that had recently opened atop an old elevated train track on the West side of Manhattan, a relative told me I must have thought of Owen upon encountering such a beautiful sight. I shook my head and said that, no, I had not thought of him at that moment. As I uttered the words, I wondered whether my sorrow was equal to the loss.

What parent will admit to one day grieving for their child until their body could no longer stand the pain, and then going out to shop? What parent will confess to resenting an eight-year-old boy who drowned in a river? What parent will declare that, while he misses raising his son, life is smoother without his stubborn defiance?

Grief is surrounded by shame as well.

Alison and I sometimes asked each other whether people were judging us. After all, we had taken a child on a rafting trip and returned without him. Ignorance breeds speculation, and few people knew exactly what had happened. We had recounted the day's events to a handful of friends and relatives, but only bits and pieces and only during the first months. When I spoke about it, my body shivered, not in a way that anyone would notice, but enough that I had to wrap my arms around my chest. So I stopped.

Now and then the faint echoes of other people's judgments reached us. Julian divulged that one of his friends had overheard a neighbor ask his mother why Owen's father had not done anything (the neighbor had heard that we ran the river on our own). One of my nieces said that she should probably not repeat what a relative had said about the accident. Her mother changed the subject, but later that day, as the girl and I took a walk in the woods around Woodstock, she told me the relative's remarks had to do with kayaking. No doubt it was something about rapids and reckless parents. I did not ask my niece for details, but noticed what she said next: "When I was scared some time ago, my parents told me they'd always be there to keep me safe."

What people told others at two or three degrees of separation could not take me to depths I had not already explored on my own. It did, however, remind me once again that I was living in a world apart. As months elapsed, friends stopped telling us about their own tragedies. The time for shared suffering had passed. In its place, there was distance, incomprehension, perhaps stigma.

When confronted with the death of a child, we need to believe that we would have behaved differently, that we would never expose our kids to such dangers. Such thoughts maintain the order of the world; they make it possible to go forward. After a fire killed three sisters and their grandparents in Connecticut, a local TV station cut to a man on the street, out with his toddler: "If I had done something like this, if I had caused the death of my son, I couldn't go on living," he said.

Perhaps the poet Lamartine was right when he wrote that only a father who, like him, had lost his only daughter could understand what he was going through. And Victor Hugo, whose verses I continued to read: "You parents who have suffered like me / Have you felt what I felt?"

Alison and I both spent time with other parents who had suffered like us and felt what we felt. We did so separately most of the time. Within a few months, I had fashioned a small circle of bereaved parents whom I saw with regularity, though never together.

The first one was an old friend and also the only one who had ever met Owen. Her toddler had died of a genetic disease a decade earlier. Sadness keeps resurfacing without warning, she said, but the sorrow evolves, the pain morphs, the body adapts. You have the right to curl up and cry, she told me, but do not allow grief to consume you. She shared her experiences while acknowledging that living through her personal horror (as she called it) still made her helpless before the death of other children, afraid of saying the wrong thing. I cherished the intimate physicality of her presence, the tender moments we now spent with her son and mine. Whenever I think of my loss, she said, I think of yours.

The second member of this circle, a man I met after the accident, is the father who told me about taking his late daughter on walks. He approached grief with startling precision, devising tangible, quantifiable markers that he shared with me. For instance: years after his daughter's death, he could give only 60 percent of himself at work. In his company, I could believe that order might persist after all. I could also confront the same intractable questions. His daughter had succumbed to a sudden illness rather than an accident, but he still spent countless hours reviewing the circumstances and the decisions he and his wife had made before her death. Had they chosen the right hospital? Had they taken their daughter there soon enough? He once told me that, regardless of the situation, guilt is unavoidable because the chain always ends with the parents. This was a summons to let go.

The last of these bereaved parents, another new friend, struck me as equally lucid and self-aware, but less linear in his thinking. Our conversations resembled Robert Altman movies, with piercing but fleeting insights, and strands crossing, interrupted, and resumed. Memories of our respective accidents surfaced, then receded, then returned. This father felt as if he were repeating himself when it came to his son's death. He also wished that people would ask direct questions instead of referring to him as the guy who lost his child. He spoke at length about the day his son died. "It just happened, that's all there is," he said. There were no lessons to be learned about the catastrophic nature of life. The notion that some things elude understanding escaped me at that time, but not the way he kept circling his own accident or the fact that, somewhere in his apartment, there was an envelope full of unseen photographs of his son. Someone had handed them to him a few days after his accident. Perhaps he would look one day, he said. His uncertainty echoed my own.

I do not expect these parents to recognize themselves—their full selves—in the descriptions I have given. I leave out so much about their grief and their layered lives and our time together. These portraits are facets of my imagined self: I project upon them my yearnings for affection, order, and raw honesty. But it is true that together we were neither culprits nor saints nor heroes—just unkempt sufferants who did not worry about unasked questions, excessive expectations, or matters best left unsaid. If my bereaved friends could talk about fading images of their child's face, then I could open up about complicated feelings toward Owen and the accident.

And yet, there were times when I felt I had unloaded too much during our conversations. While we all needed to derive something from these encounters, it was not necessarily the same thing. We could not always be ready to traverse barren lands together. Sometimes, one of us dragged the other into a place that, for whatever reason, proved inhospitable that day. At other times, I realized that I was not truly listening, not fully present. Part of me, 40 percent perhaps, remained elsewhere. And there was only so much I could say, even to them, about the river.

Is this why, toward the end of the first year, I found myself in the basement of a church, seated in a circle with other men and women who had lost children? Underground, there are rooms full of anonymous people who rarely encounter others like them in their everyday lives. All of these people are their own worst nightmares.

I would probably have attended this support group earlier if not for the bereaved couple, both in their fifties, who visited us in New York soon after the accident. A drunk driver had slammed into their daughter's car two years earlier. Afterward they had turned away from the world; anger had led to isolation. They still went to work, but there was no cooking, no music or art, no hobbies save for workouts, no laughing, no conversations that did not revolve around their loss. The wife sat erect and spoke about all this with resolve; the husband slumped and said little. Both concurred that life was bleak and would remain so, without solace besides the company of other bereaved parents. They had no friends outside the support group because no one else could understand.

This couple had come to warn us about what lay in store and welcome us into the universe they inhabited. Alison and I heard their consoling words, but not as loudly as their rancor. Neither one of us imagined it possible to live the rest of our lives closed off from a world that bore the stain of collective guilt. We did not say this; instead, we strung together platitudes about walks and friends and remaining open to different experiences. As I watched this couple drive away, I pictured them telling one another that, once the shock wore off, Alison and I would come to accept our new reality.

This visit proved so chilling that, for many months, I stayed away from the support group. And then one evening, I ended up in a church basement with fifty other bereaved parents. We went around the room and introduced ourselves and our dead children. It was a litany of tragedy: the elderly father whose son had overdosed; the middle-aged Serbian mother whose daughter had died of cancer; the white-haired woman who presented her only son as her best friend; the composed father with a long face whose two boys had drowned on the same day (his wife sat quietly by his side, hands clasped on her lap); the elegant gentleman whose son had collapsed while playing basketball; the young Hispanic woman who could not utter her daughter's name; and me, the father whose son had slipped away on a river. This collective recitation defies comprehension, but in this circle it seemed almost normal.

After the introductions, we broke up into subgroups: mothers, fathers, recent deaths, parents of suicides, and other categories that could vary from one meeting to the next. The qualities that govern the world outside this basement—age, income, race—had little purchase here, except for gender. I went with the fathers.

A fast-speaking man told us that his wife had refused to mention their seven-year-old son for two decades after his death. There were no pictures, no stories, no memories in their home. But one day his wife's sister lost her son, and then the pictures came out.

A young man with dreadlocks said that grief is like carrying a heavy bag that people stop noticing. Others proposed different metaphors. I am an amputee who still walks, but no longer in the same way. A nuclear bomb has gone off in my home. Grief is like a brick in my pocket, which I can touch at any time. It is a chronic disease, with flare-ups and periods of remission. These were clichés once again, but full of pathos—desperate attempts to make life fit within some kind of symbolic scheme.

A war veteran was so angry that he would explode, he said, if he did not attend meetings. The father to my right wanted to know if anyone else had been told to get on with his life. It had only been three months, he said.

Some faces became recognizable after a few meetings, but there were always new ones, or else silent folk who suddenly unveiled some new torment. One evening, it was a big guy in his thirties, with alert but tired eyes. He asked the group if anyone knew about layovers. No one did—not in this context—so he explained. It is when a parent sleeps with a baby and accidentally suffocates it by rolling onto its body. The man spoke at a measured clip, his emotions in check. He had been napping with his infant son, woke up, let his wife take his place, and left for work. His wife fell asleep and rolled over. Some of their relatives could not forgive, he said.

I talked to the fathers about my guilt and asked them about theirs. They all seemed to sit up in their chairs, even those who said they never felt guilty. A man in a gray suit, his nails chewed to the skin, told us about his daughter, who had died of a rare disease at the age of three. He continued to feel the guilt—"the father's philosophical guilt," he called it.

We only skimmed the surface, and yet it was for such words and stories that I came back—for jolts of reality that pushed against the boundaries of human existence. This made me feel alive in the realm of the dead.

Still, after half a dozen meetings, I stepped away from this room. I did so because, beneath the diversity of voices and experiences, I kept encountering the all-too-seductive notion that our lot was without equal. At each meeting, someone spoke about the slights and perplexed gazes bereaved parents face every day. A few of the people I met had been attending meetings for a decade and only socialized with bereaved parents because those whom they called civilians could never get it. "Your entire address book changes," a coordinator told me.

This community could have become mine. In fact, I sometimes felt the urge to take up permanent residence there. But if I acted upon it, could I exist as anything but a bereaved father? Could I escape anger and the melancholy that, as the Roman philosopher Seneca put it, feeds upon its very bitterness while turning grief into a morbid pleasure?

And could I imagine a life without Alison? She accompanied me to one meeting and never returned. Seneca once counseled a bereaved mother against "that most perverse distinction, that of being considered the most unhappy of women." Alison arrived at this conclusion on her own. Living in seclusion and rejecting people for what they could not understand would destroy her, she said.

FOURTEEN

Ella: *Where were you when it happened?*

The people for whom I longed—available whenever I needed them, still open to the world, ready to share their experiences without expecting me to reciprocate—did not exist, at least not anywhere I could see. To find such bereaved parents, I had to canvass other centuries. An important part of my mourning that first year took place in eras other than my own.

I had begun with Victor Hugo but found others. In the Renaissance, the astrologer Nostradamus lost his wife and two children to the plague epidemic that devastated Provence in the 1530s. While he mourned them privately, this ordeal allowed him to touch and capture in poetic prophecies the suffering and disquiet that so many of his contemporaries felt during those tumultuous times. Across the English Channel, Ben Jonson and Shakespeare expressed their sorrow for their departed sons in harrowing verses. "My sin was too much hope of thee, loved boy," Jonson wrote. "Seven years thou wert lent to me." Shakespeare included a bereaved mother in *King John*, the first play he wrote after his son's death in 1596. "Grief fills the room of my absent child, / Lies in his bed, walks up and down with me."

While some of these bereaved parents had attained fame, most were ordinary folk who had left a record of their suffering. Around 1800, a Burgundian notary by the name of Jean-Baptiste Boniard lost two of his children, including his five-year-old daughter Adèle, who succumbed to scarlet fever. He kept a detailed account of his last conversation with the girl, the "rosebud" who liked to kiss and comfort her father and died while reciting a fable to him. I found this out by chance, while reading the reminiscences of his grandson. Boniard was a fascinating character (local politician, journalist, amateur archaeologist and astronomer), but his relationship with his late daughter told me everything I wanted to know about him.

Decades later, Victorian parents mounted images of deceased children on matchboxes with "lovely little scrolls" and snippets of hair. Charles Darwin kept objects that had belonged to his daughter Anna, as well as her writings, in a box that he built. The English widower John Horsley said he felt better when he wrote about the four sons and daughter he had lost to illness. The American Henry Bowditch, father of a soldier who died in Virginia in 1863, recovered his son's body and then compiled memorial volumes and scrapbooks about his life. This is not how men were expected to grieve. Bowditch understood this, but he maintained his course. "The labor was a sweet one," he wrote. "It took me out of myself."

And the Englishwoman Janet Trevelyan—she wrote everything she could recall about her son Theo after his death in 1911: "I know that as we get further from the pain of these last days the pure joy and beauty of his little life will shine out more and more and will be like a light in our hearts to illuminate the rest of our way."

My investigations of the past were in character: as a historian, this is what I had done every day for years. Uncovering such narratives, memorials, and poems came instinctively, proof that some part of my professional self remained intact.

But there was nothing scholarly about this exploration, no questions to resolve about grief across the centuries. Historians are wary of their biases and tend to keep their emotions and proclivities at a remove from their research. I now found this impossible. It was companionship I sought. I wanted to *know* these men and women who, as Horsley put it, kept "the uncertainty of this life ever in view." They inhabited a realm of pure emotion and allowed me to join them, to mourn in their company whenever I so desired.

W. E. B. Du Bois had faced uncharted expanses upon burying his son, in 1899. "It seemed a ghostly unreal day—the wraith of life," he wrote. "We seemed to rumble down an unknown street." Granville Stanley Hall, the American founder of gerontology in the nineteenth century, felt that the death of his daughter by gas asphyxiation was "the greatest bereavement of my life—such a one, indeed, as rarely falls to the lot of man." Hall was forty-four, but this great fatigue, as he called it, made him feel much older. I rumbled down unknown streets with Du Bois and Hall, prey to a great fatigue that made me feel as old as they had.

Except for those Hugo poems, I did not tell Alison of my explorations. I did not require her presence alongside men and women with whom I could commune day and night, all of us part of a community that remained perpetually accessible.

This quest also took me to World War II, with its untold number of dead children. For Jewish parents in Nazi-occupied Europe, the loss of a child was both swallowed up and magnified by the attack upon entire communities. The Polish shoemaker Simon

Powsinoga withstood one form of degradation after another in the Warsaw Ghetto, but not the death of his only son. "Two days ago I was still a human being, . . . I could support my own family and even help others," he said in the midst of the war. "I just don't care now. I don't have Mates, what's the point of living?"

This despair provided little succor, but there was no way around World War II in my family. My childhood in Brussels had been colored by the story of my maternal grandparents as a young couple during the war. I had always viewed Zosia and Jules as embodiments of History. When I was a child, their everyday lives seemed normal enough. They dressed in the morning and ate breakfast as I did; they walked on the same sidewalks; they gossiped and quarreled and laughed like everyone else. But they had experienced something I had not; their proximity to danger and death had made them different *kinds* of people.

Zosia had grown up in an affluent Jewish family in Warsaw. Her father, a silk merchant whose business took him to France and Belgium, was sufficiently lucid about the rise of anti-Semitism to move his wife and children to Brussels in 1932. It was there that Zosia met Jules, a diamond trader who would see action as a Belgian conscript in 1940 and then spend a year in Germany as a prisoner of war. They married in March 1942, and left for Southern France two months later. The French collaborationist regime in Vichy, and especially the Italian troops that controlled the city of Nice, seemed more forgiving than the Nazis who occupied Belgium. After an epic journey by train, bus, and foot, my grandparents arrived in Nice and registered as foreigners with the French police. Afterward, they rented an apartment and plotted their next step. My grandmother was pregnant.

When Owen died, Jules was long dead and Zosia in the throes of dementia. And yet one of the first things I did, without awareness, was to summon them to my side. I did so on the river, when

I recited the Shema in their company, and back home, when I returned to their wartime story. Although my grandparents had been dehumanized and persecuted, although our experiences were by no means similar, we could now enter a different realm of existence and encounter together shock and sorrow, and perhaps resilience. There was empathy, too. My grandparents knew too much about human frailty and the contingency of everyday life to ask me the kinds of questions I was asking myself, such as, How could you have allowed this to happen? How could you have let Owen go?

The accident changed something else in the way I saw my grandparents. After all, they had survived the war with their infant daughter—my mother.

Shortly after arriving in Nice, they were arrested by the French police and sent to the detention camp of Rivesaltes, near the Pyrenees mountains. They were unlikely to remain there for long. With the Germans about to take possession of Rivesaltes from the French, prisoners were being transferred to other camps or deported to Auschwitz. Zosia wrote to an official whom she had met at the Nice police station and asked him to intervene. He did. My grandparents were freed in November 1942. They returned to Nice, where my mother was born a month later.

The official, Charles, remained present in their lives. He warned them about imminent arrests and helped them find an apartment. He also introduced them to his wife, Annie. The two couples sometimes socialized, strolling together in public parks and posing for snapshots. In one photograph, Annie and Charles cozy up with Zosia on a bench, like long-lost cousins. In another, Annie cradles the swaddled baby in her arms. The child remains at the center of things. Annie and Charles kept her for several months in the fall of 1943, when massive round-ups of Jews forced my grandparents into hiding. My mother's first name, Francine, serves as a tangible reminder of this time and place—France and Nice intermingled. Her middle name is her godmother's: Annie.

Why had Charles helped this couple while, I assumed (rightly or not), stamping papers and contributing to the bureaucratic machine of identification, surveillance, and deportation? After the war, my grandmother made allowances and expressed gratitude for the man who had saved their lives, but never spoke much about his wife despite the risks she had taken. While my grandparents often vacationed in Nice, they only introduced my mother to her godparents twice, once when she was five and once when she was seventeen, in 1959.

It may be impossible to know what transpired among the four of them, but this did not stop me from conjuring up scenarios after Owen's death: a social divide, infidelity or attraction, shame, jealousy, competing affections for the baby. At some point, it dawned on me that my grandparents might have kept a distance from a couple who reminded them of their interrupted youth and a truth that is not always easy to accept: how much we owe to others when our life veers out of control.

My mother could not understand why I asked her for more information about her parents and the war. It's a simple story, she said, and she may have been right. But I saw complicated and perhaps conflicted human beings whose behavior transcended the binary categories—in this case rescue and collaboration, justice and ingratitude—with which we all too often make sense of the world. Ultimately, it was impossible to determine what a savior looked like, or who exactly had saved whom.

Zosia seemed to understand these ambiguities. "Things are never entirely positive," she once told me regarding Charles, "and they are never entirely negative either." In this respect as well, my grandparents—the grandparents I imagined—provided solace and companionship. Together, we could escape the expectations of others and absolute conceptions of virtuous behavior.

But for how long? When Zosia recalled her wartime years, she described Jules's forays into the black market. On some days, he would return with bananas for the baby, and only for the baby because that is all they had. She also depicted herself as an ingenious woman who made her own luck, took risks, and never allowed fear to hold her back. She had reached out to Charles as he sat behind his desk; later, she had written him from Rivesaltes. Someone had saved my grandparents, but according to this family story, they, too, had saved themselves and their daughter.

So, the three of us did not inhabit the same realm, after all. My grandparents were not only rescuees, but also rescuers and parents who had fulfilled their responsibilities. Luck had played its part, but this was not the main takeaway. Their story could not be mine.

During a trip to Brussels a few months after the accident, I paid a visit to my grandmother's first cousin Ginette. She was the only surviving relative who might know something about these wartime events. Ginette's father and Zosia's had been brothers and business partners in Belgium before the war, although Zosia's alone managed to bring his family out of Warsaw. When war broke out, Ginette found herself in the ghetto with her mother, her polio-stricken sister, and her husband. The mother and sister were shot on the spot; the husband perished later. Ginette was deported to the concentration camp of Majdanek in central Poland and then to an ammunition plant and from there to Bergen-Belsen in Germany. She worked in the latrines and somehow survived detention and typhus. "One gets used to anything," she once told my mother. After the war, she settled in Brussels and married an Auschwitz survivor.

Ginette was impeccably dressed the day I came by. Everything was impeccable in her apartment: the rows of books, the coffee she served, the paintings full of melancholy. She listened as I told her about Charles and Annie but had nothing to impart because she had never heard about them. It was not a question of memory: even at eighty-three, hers remained sharp. After the war, she said, all surviving Jews felt that they had suffered in exceptional ways. What others had withstood proved irrelevant. As for non-Jews, they were so caught up in their own hardships— lost youth, hunger, cold, deprivation—that they deemed all wartime suffering equivalent. Everyone had gone through bad times. Why should your hardship take precedence over mine? Zosia must have encountered the same responses, Ginette said. This would explain why she had never brought up Charles and Annie.

I thought of another possibility: Zosia may not have known how to speak about such things with a cousin who had survived Nazi extermination camps. I once heard Zosia say that deportees (such as Ginette) had done what they had to do in order to survive. It was impossible to know what had happened in those camps, she said. Her remark did not strike me as free of judgment.

As she refilled our cups, Ginette asked me to share anything I might uncover about this official. She seemed to mean it, although I could not really tell. But it no longer mattered because my thoughts were now floating between Zosia and Owen, between Owen and the Warsaw Ghetto, between Owen and Ginette after Bergen-Belsen. If I had paid Ginette a visit, it was also to encounter a person who had endured something I could not imagine and to learn something about corners of human experience that resist understanding.

I wanted to ask Ginette about life with dead siblings and dead parents and dead children. But she had not mentioned Owen when I arrived, and after an hour she still had not uttered his name. She talked at length about her dog's health, but not a word about Owen. The longer we spoke, the more difficult it became to think of anything but this silence. As I said, her memory was sharp.

When the sun began to set, Ginette walked me to the door. As she took my coat out of the closet, her dog sniffed my shoes. Ginette explained that the animal was distressed because her longtime caretaker, an illegal immigrant, had been expelled from Belgium.

"Your dog senses things," I said. "She can tell that I am distressed as well."

Ginette looked at me in surprise. "You're distressed as well?"

My final attempt to secure something from Ginette had fallen flat. Her silence could not be an oversight; it was too glaring given the circumstances. I could only make sense of it in relation to her silence about her wartime ordeal. As far as I knew, she rarely talked about that period, perhaps because it would overwhelm her or because she had come to see her experience as nontransferable. Since she did not offer lessons, I told myself that she may have been teaching by example. The only thing to do was to watch her imprint order upon her life, master her emotions, and carry on without her sister, mother, and first husband—and no doubt with them as well, even if, like Owen, they had to remain in the background. Ginette was a concentration camp survivor; she bore the loss of these people and others—the entire world of her youth—but she was also a mother, a businesswoman, and a voracious reader whose shelves were stacked with novels by authors of all nationalities. Literature retains faith in life and humanity; it remains open to the varieties of human experience.

I clung to this lesson about the living and the dead after my visit. But I also knew how much I craved guidance of any sort. Like Ginette, I would have to find a way on my own.

FIFTEEN

Henry: *Where did this happen?*

We had booked a trip on the Green without knowing anything about the river—its name, its topography, the path it cut across Utah and Colorado, or even the nature of its rapids. The outfitters' brochure had advertised the vacation as family fun for first-time rafters and children, a bonding experience. This seemed ideal for novices like us. Having signed up for a journey into a foreign, antediluvian landscape, we did not need to know more about the waterway or the region. I already spent so much of my professional life immersed in research that I resisted reading up beforehand. Doing so would have spoiled the inherent strangeness of the place.

Had I consulted but one book or website, though, I would have learned that the rapids on which we ended up had a dramatic history. Over the past two centuries, Native American tribes, trappers, explorers, dam engineers, river runners, and kayakers have come together in these waters. I know this because, not long after the accident, I began collecting information on the Green. What started as an episodic probe rapidly turned into an all-consuming inquiry. I downloaded articles, mined databases, called the Utah Bureau of Land Management, and pored over expedition reports, travel accounts, and geological surveys. In the tent, I had felt nothing but hatred toward that river. Afterward, I could not let go. The Green and its history beckoned with irresistible force.

I never gave my name when making these calls, and never told my friends what I was doing with my time. Local experts, I feared, might scorn the New York City father who had lost his son in rapids he did not master. Friends might ask innocuous but unanswerable questions about what I expected to uncover. It was difficult to tell anyone—including Julian and Alison, who said she had left the river behind—that I hoped to understand how we had found ourselves in that precise spot. A natural and human history might just explain what had been possible and what had not been on that day. Each new detail, each precedent, each anecdote might just draw me closer to the truth of a river that, like the other protagonists in this story, was not evil but could not be fully innocent either.

The Green River has not always held that name. The Crow tribes who inhabited its headwaters in Wyoming called it Prairie Hen River. The Ute and Snakes referred to it as Bitterroot. In the late eighteenth century, Spanish explorers called its lower reach Rio Verde, perhaps because of the moss and lichen and brush reflected on the surface. The first person to call it Green River (in English, this time) was reportedly a beaver trapper named William Ashley, in 1825. The name stuck. Washington Irving depicted the Green as a "mere mountain torrent, dashing northward over crag and precipice, in a succession of cascades." Nothing about its color: it is the force of the current that matters.

The Green surges from Wyoming's Wind River Mountains, flows through sagebrush flats, veers east to avert the Uinta range, skims the edge of Colorado, slopes southwest, and finally plunges 450 miles across Utah, all the way to Cataract Canyon, where it throws itself into the Colorado River. After entering Utah, it winds through the Browns Park wetlands, a bird sanctuary that was once inhabited by Ute and Shoshoni tribes as well as cattlemen, homesteaders, stockmen, rustlers, cattle thieves, and outlaws like Butch Cassidy and the Sundance Kid. It was a good place in which to live and hide.

Afterward, the Green enters Dinosaur National Monument, 200,000 acres of wilderness that Woodrow Wilson incorporated into the National Park System in 1915. Here, the river squeezes into a canyon that seems to have sprouted out of nowhere. This is a land of red Precambrian rock formations and grottoes. John Wesley Powell, the explorer who led the first expedition down the river in 1869, wrote that "the vermilion gleams and roseate hues, blending with the green and gray tints, are slowly changing to somber brown." While facing the cliffs and the narrow channel ahead, one member of his party suggested they name the canyon Lodore, after an English poem that speaks of water "rushing and flushing and brushing and gushing."

As his expedition approached Lodore, Powell wrote: "Now it is a dark portal to a region of gloom—the gateway through which we are to enter on our voyage of exploration tomorrow. What shall we find?"

Of Powell's many expeditions out West, none was as ambitious as the one he launched to solve the "last geographical problem of the U.S., that of the canyons of the Green and Colorado Rivers." While the Green's lower and upper ends were known, no one had explored its interior section.

Powell was a natural scientist, chair of geology at Normal

State University in Illinois, who sported a beard and wore jeans and boots out West. He also designed his own boats for the expedition, three oak vessels with double sterns and watertight compartments for supplies. It is not clear, however, that he understood what he was getting into. He had never run a rapid before, and neither had the party of fur hunters, college students, and soldiers who embarked on this thousand-mile journey across inhospitable territory.

Still, the early days went fine. Strapped to a chair on the lead boat, Powell scouted the river and shouted commands to the oarsmen, who, as was customary, faced upstream. He waived a red flag to show the other two boats what route to follow. If difficulties arose, they would have time to alter their course or else pull to shore.

Two weeks into the trip, Powell's party entered the Canyon of Lodore. Powell wrote that the water sometimes "descends with a smooth, unruffled surface," and then it tumbles "in a channel filled with dangerous rocks that break the waves into whirlpools." Trouble came on a series of rapids that dropped thirty-five feet in a little over a half mile. This was more than the Grand Canyon, more than Cataract Canyon, and much more than what they had encountered thus far (the river had been dropping twenty-two feet per mile).

This stretch consisted of two steep descents, each one fifteen feet in height, with water coming in through narrow channels and boulders that were fully or partially hidden under what another observer called "a continuous sheet of boiling foam." At the upper fall, water flowed on both sides of a small island; at the lower fall, the current ran into the canyon wall and a cliff that came in at a right angle. The Green had no choice but to cut a channel in the limestone, resurfacing two hundred feet below.

As they approached the upper falls, Powell gave the signal

to disembark and portage, that is, to carry the crafts and cargo over land. For some reason—perhaps the rapids' intensity, perhaps high boulders—his red flag went unseen. One of the boats, the *No-Name*, smashed into rocks and broke apart, propelling three of the men into the waters. They scrambled to the islet, now known as No-Name Island. No casualties, but the boat and its contents were lost.

"We adopt the name Disaster Falls," Powell wrote, "for the scene of so much peril and loss."

The party carried on through Lodore and then to the Colorado without further mishaps. Powell gained fame as an explorer who published his story of peril, loss, and survival with the Smithsonian in 1875: *Report on the Exploration of the Colorado River of the West and Its Tributaries*. He soon became a mainstay of American lore. "An incredible adventure story," Tony Hillerman wrote of one recent book on the expedition.

Is that all it was? Were the stories of the Green and Disaster Falls nothing but tales of adventure? Delving into lesser-known corners of this history, I compiled a running list, a kind of police blotter of mishaps and near misses at Disaster Falls. The entries loomed larger alongside one another.

1932   A seven-member party traveling from Wyoming to Green River, Utah, loses a boat "while negotiating the leap over Disaster Falls." The passengers are safe.

1934   Employees of Utah's Fish and Game Department crash at the entrance of the falls. A passenger almost drowns, but a river runner grabs the line at the end of the boat and pulls him to shore

1938   River runner Norman Nevills attempts to slip through

Upper Disaster, but one of his boats gets caught on a rock. As he tries to dislodge it with ropes, "a terrific current shoved the water right down my throat and choked me." His party makes it out, but it is a close call.

1949   Two college students and a lab technician lose one of their plywood boats after it capsizes.

1951   An expedition of engineers, scientists, photographers, and representatives of the Colorado Game and Fish Commission crashes two boats. A river runner is caught under water; some passengers fall overboard and cling to a boat through a mile and a half of rapids. Afterward, they feel like "a group of men who had gone into the valley of death and returned."

People got into trouble on the Green during these decades because the river was becoming a recreational area. One of the first men to run it for fun in the late 1800s had introduced a forward-facing rowing technique that made it possible to traverse rapids that Powell had had to portage. By the early 1930s, local "piloting dudes" were making a little cash as river runners for adventurous travelers.

One of these runners, a local builder and outdoorsman named Bus Hatch, launched commercial trips in 1932. His wooden boats could only carry one or two passengers, however, and they sometimes split after hitting boulders. A solution emerged after World War II, when the U.S. Army made its surplus rubber rafts available commercially. These cheap inflatable devices, which required little maintenance, could hold up to fifteen passengers in relative comfort and proved easy to manoeuver in waves and holes. Hatch introduced six-day rafting packages for families and large parties. In 1953, Dinosaur National Monument awarded him its first river concession permit. Soon, there were a dozen operators and close to twenty thousand people on the river every year. It is here, on the rapids of the Green, that whitewater rafting and commercial tourism first came together.

These rafts seem to have reduced the number of spills. In the early 1950s, a local newspaper referred to Disaster Falls as "a boulder-choked spume of rapids," but praised Hatch "for the few accidents that have occurred with large groups being taken down the rivers." Passengers would disembark at the top of Upper Disaster and walk to the foot of the rapids. Only the most foolhardy rafted this section. A Sierra Club party that included toddlers and old ladies came out of "the tumbling cataracts of dread Lodore soaked and battered and happy." I assume that they portaged Disaster Falls.

The most important change in this environmental history occurred in 1964, with the opening of the Flaming Gorge dam and reservoir fifty miles upstream. Whereas warm and silty water had previously swelled in the spring depending on snow accumulation, the dam now let out a steady flow, cold and clear. This transformed the river's ecology, with dire consequences for wildlife, but it also controlled the rush of rapids that had proved daunting for so long. Today, the Green runs on average between 800 and 4,700 cubic feet per second—considerably less than the 24,000 cubic feet that Powell faced.

Disaster Falls, in short, is no longer much of a fall. But it remains disastrous. It is between Upper and Lower Disaster that Owen drowned.

What can history do after this?

On some days, I considered counterfactuals and allowed myself to believe that events could have unfolded differently. *Belknap's Waterproof Dinosaur River Guide* explains that, in the

1950s, a proposed dam at Echo Park, near the boat launch at which our trip ended, would have destroyed an entire ecosystem on the Green and the Yampa rivers. Had environmentalists not defeated the project, water would have flooded gorges, creeks, wetlands, and cottonwood groves. Disaster Falls and other rapids would have vanished as well. "But O would be alive," I scribbled in the margin.

On other days, I looked into the evolution of safety regulation on that stretch of the river. This was not an easy thing to do—I could find only bits of evidence—but I did learn that Dinosaur National Monument required permits and liability insurance in the late 1950s. Independent-minded runners such as Hatch, long entrusted with maintenance and rescues on the river, did not take such regulation well. By the 1970s, two seasonal rangers watched over the campgrounds and intervened when vacationers ran into trouble. The Park Service also reduced the number of rafters permitted on the river by half. Perhaps it did so for safety reasons, but mostly, it seems, the thousands of tourists were harming the environment.

When I called the Dinosaur river office in search of archival records about Disaster Falls, a manager told me there weren't any. To gain clarity, I turned to kayakers who had recently run the rapids and written about them. Some deemed the stretch harmless. It was "an easy run," one environmentalist recounted a year before our accident. "The rapids we faced this afternoon don't much resemble the ferocious falls that sundered the *No-Name*." I felt relief upon reading his words: they suggested that we had not dropped Owen into an impossible place.

But if Disaster Falls had been reengineered into a harmless ride, why had we fared so poorly? Why hadn't I done better on that easy run?

Rereading the material I had collected, I now latched onto the perils that boaters continue to face. The *Vernal Express*, a local newspaper, warned in 1954 that "light craft and unskilled guides may spell disaster when such groups approach the many places in the canyons where the river becomes a churned-up demon of destruction and terror." These words were written before the dam's construction, I knew this, but the environmentalist who later depicted Disaster as an easy run similarly claimed that the new dam at Flaming Gorge had turned the Green into "a machine with teeth of stone." I took note.

One day, I discovered a blog by an outdoorsman who had spent thirty years running the major rivers of the West. His takeaway is that Disaster Falls remains treacherous because currents converge into a narrow channel with a huge rock in the middle. The biggest danger in such situations, he wrote, is to wrap one's boat. This happens when one hits a rock sideways and the current bears down with too much force to allow any movement. "Wrapping is worse than flipping the boat upside down," the blogger went on, "because it can be virtually impossible to free a boat that wraps on a mid-stream rock."

Beneath the surface of the Green, a churned-up demon of destruction and terror continues to lurk. For a while, this gave me another kind of solace. It explained why amateur boaters could deem Disaster Falls runnable and then find themselves overmatched, pinned against rocks in their kayaks and duckies.

And yet, this story about Disaster Falls had its own dark side. Alison and I had brought our sons to a notorious place whose name had long served as a warning. And we had had no clue. Wallace Stegner wrote that "nearly everyone who runs any part of the canyons now—and they are many thousands each year— either carries this story of Powell's in his duffel bag or has it read or recited to him around the fire."

Not us. During the bus ride from the hotel to the river on the morning of the accident, I was not reading Powell but rather Joseph Mitchell's *Up in the Old Hotel*, a book about all-but-forgotten slices of New York City history. I knew too little about the Green to even anticipate a region of gloom on our own voyage of exploration. Did the other members of our party know about Powell's expedition? The traveler from San Francisco, the Las Vegas police officer who had come with her two children, did they know? That morning on the bus, I did not spot them reading about the Gold Rush or the first casinos in Nevada.

It is possible that the guides planned to recite this story of Powell's after dinner that night, but we never made it to the campfire.

The final character in this history is Colin Fletcher, the founding father of American wilderness backpacking. In 1989, Fletcher hiked and rafted the entire length of the Green and Colorado rivers on his own and then wrote a book about it. Like others before him, he ended up at Disaster Falls. While scouting the rapids, he recalled the crash of the *No-Name* and considered potential outcomes. I read his account several times, my mood fluctuating according to the words I chose to underline on that day.

Sometimes, I saw a run that Fletcher deemed passable: *If this was as straightforward and unimpeded as it looked, probably no problem* . . . . *The whole thing looked very runnable.* . . . *Not at all a scary business.*

At other times, I saw rapids that harbored hidden dangers: *But if that torrent thick-souping through the chute concealed any obstacles.* . . . *The undertow could suck you under and pin you there, helpless.*

Fletcher's account could go either way. It could mean anything, so it might as well have meant nothing. This is what I came to feel about history as well. I had spent so much time trying to determine whether we had run the same waters as Powell; I had invested the question with so much urgency. At some point, however, I had to acknowledge that the falls would always prove as disastrous as I wanted them to be. History could provide neither explanations nor release.

And yet, history lived on as my personal obsession, comparable to Alison's compulsive walking. Perhaps this is what we all need in the wake of catastrophic losses, some means of channeling the manic energy and conflicted yearnings that well up within us. After his son's death, a friend of mine took up martial arts and became a black belt.

History also endured as presence: the history I wished I had known, the history that might have led us to make different decisions on rapids that never seemed as safe as we were told. I could now open myself to the signs that, inscribed within the rocks and sands of the Green, make it clear that these storied falls could suddenly turn tragic.

History channeled, finally, the mythic power of a place in and out of time, a place whose primeval force had pulled us in and pushed us forward in ways I might never fully understand but could now feel. Owen and I came together within a history of nature and civilization that neither began nor ended on the day of his death. What took place that afternoon could have faded into oblivion, an event effaced by the same catastrophic forces that, as Owen and I knew too well, had wiped out Talman Street in Brooklyn.

Still, Owen stands alone. Alison, Julian, and I had been there on the Green, we had taken part in this history, but he is the one who joined William Ashley, John Wesley Powell, Bus Hatch, and Colin Fletcher on a river that cut across Dinosaur National Monument, rushed through the Canyon of Lodore, and twisted itself into a series of rapids that, regardless of the dam and re-gardless of the flow, will always bear and deserve the name of Disaster Falls.

PART

II

The Place of the Dead

SIXTEEN

*Iris: Was Owen eight turning nine
or nine turning ten?*

want to write that after a full year of grief, after watching
a child die and uncovering hidden suffering around me, I
led a life of heightened kindness. This is not what happened,
but I want to write that it did because this would ward off the
notion that the father still standing at the end of that year was
a slightly older but otherwise undistinguishable version of the
one who had left New York for Utah with two children and
returned with one. *Something* had to come out of this.

In nineteenth-century England, Anglican tracts presented the
death of a child as a "providential dispensation," a kind of spiritual challenge for the parent's soul. One of them asked grieving
parents, "Are you really willing that this affliction should prove
really beneficial? Are you willing to be improved by it?" I was
more than willing, not out of religious leanings, but due to an
ingrained belief in progress and personal growth: each year better than the next; life as a series of experiences that yield insights
into oneself and others; at the very least, a little less pain each
day. Owen's death had weakened, but not extinguished, this belief. Alongside grief, intertwined with it, there was now a fear of
decline and the intolerable suspicion that things were returning

to the way they had been except for the fact that one of our sons was gone.

"A Nearness to Tremendousness—An Agony Procures," Emily Dickinson wrote. "By a departing light / We see acuter, quite." But the emotional acuity of the early months petered out with the light that second year. The tension and wakefulness that gave my days such density, the immersion in a fleeting present, the molecular awareness of fragility, the exposure to the pain of others: all of this slowly faded. It did not entirely vanish, since I continued to consider the possibility that the men and women who surrounded me carried their own unspoken losses. But people can only spend so much time in the company of dead children. Even close friends seldom inquired now about my internal state, perhaps fearing that if I was not thinking about Owen at that moment, the question would upset what they saw as a delicate equilibrium.

To be fair, my cues remained contradictory. As Julian's bar mitzvah approached, sixteen months after the accident, Alison and I resolved to celebrate one son while finding a place for the other. I would have to be a father to both that day, rejoicing with Julian while remaining with Owen, a task that on many days seemed insurmountable. Alison and I threw a party that evening and danced late into the night, as if to invite our guests into some kind of collective release.

But when friends emailed us the next day about the beaming smiles on our faces, and when, a few weeks later, a colleague told me that he and others were beginning to see me again as a historian rather than a mourner, I did not feel relief. I feared this return to normalcy—having to become the friend and the professional I used to be. What would happen to the father who lived off the map of human experience?

And what about Julian? Alison and I believed him when he

said that Owen's death was not as hard for him as it was for us, but we also saw him break down in tears because he felt lonely. Julian told us he was forgetting the sound of Owen's voice, and that he could feel happy and sad at the same time. It was impossible to tell him how to resolve quandaries that continued to confound us.

A few weeks before his bar mitzvah, Julian showed us a poem he had written for the service. Entitled "Owen," it made no pretense that all was fine. The person whom he missed more than any other was not coming back. "Above us hangs an uncertain gloom," he wrote. "Everyone knows there is an elephant in the room. . . . My bar mitzvah is just a day, a day that I have no one with whom to play." Julian would plunge to these depths with his assembled relatives and friends and then pull them up. "Thank you for keeping us alive from the sharp pain. Today is our day, do as you see fit."

When the day came and Julian recited his verses, standing alone in the middle of the room, I allowed myself to think that the river might not prevail after all. Though nature had swept Owen away, culture—poetry and ritual, community and meaning—might still reassert itself. But the bar mitzvah was just a day; grief retained its inward pull and this more than anything else made Emily Dickinson's acuity flicker.

There were now moments when I embraced the persona of the bereaved parent, as if by virtue of my suffering I could inhabit a higher plane of existence, above the tawdry contests and unrealized ambitions of our material world. Melancholy veered all too easily into a moral superiority that blunted my sense of empathy and my curiosity about others. This was the cruelest outcome—coupled with the distance I now kept from children.

I did not inquire about the children of my friends. I did not ask my sister about her pregnancy. I did not always smile back when a kid smiled at me in the street.

Other things continued to feel meaningless: political debates, intellectual questions, and my work, too. I still could not muster much interest. But when I learned that a book contract with a leading publisher would not come through, I bent over in my office. I actually bent over because of the setback, and because I realized right then that experiencing one tragedy does not mean that more hardship will not come your way. At that moment, I had to admit that somewhere within me material strivings remained strong enough to make me bend over in disappointment. After all this?

Sometime after the one-year mark, I noticed that my right forearm no longer bore traces of the gash I had incurred while searching for Owen along the river. During the first months, I had scratched at the red scab to keep a permanent incision, a memento in the flesh, a bodily deformation that I and others would see every day. But a pink scar had emerged in its stead, and then that scar had quietly blended into the skin. I searched for it under the hair and the freckles, but there was nothing to be found. My arm looked perfectly normal.

What I am trying to say is that the second year was not easier than the first.

SEVENTEEN

Zara: *Was the water deep?*

And yet something changed at the end of that year. It happened after I invited my father on a trip to his parents' native Belarus. Over the years, Berl had collected all kinds of documents relating to his family history, among them, census records, lists of taxpayers, ship manifests, certificates of arrival, and petitions for naturalization. He kept some in the envelopes in which they arrived, lending the project a vaguely fetishistic quality. But though he often spoke of visiting Belarus, he had never followed through. Sometimes he voiced concerns about the country's repressive apparatus, but I wondered if he was afraid of going on his own. With his eightieth birthday approaching, I told him that he had to visit Belarus. I would come along, I said, and we would take Julian, too.

I did not overthink the matter, but neither could I forget that after contemplating the rapids at Disaster Falls, I had allowed the guides to override my instincts. This time, I had to trust my gut feeling; we had to go, even if the journey to the old country struck me as a little hackneyed, with its well-worn itineraries and tour companies bearing names such as Routes to Roots. The timing was poor, too. There were now days when I understood why some bereaved parents spoke about *feeding* their grief because it was the last connection to their child. The thought of traveling to a repressive, quasi-Soviet state, so far from Owen, in search of ancestors I had barely known, held little appeal.

My father's relationship to our family history complicated matters as well. Three years earlier, he had given my sister and me a CD containing sixty photographs, arranged chronologically. It began in Bobruisk, a predominantly Jewish town near Minsk that had taken advantage of its location on the Berezina River to become a trading center in the nineteenth century. After the outbreak of World War I, one of its residents, a young blacksmith named Leib Gerschowitz, deserted the Russian army and made his way to New York via Rotterdam. He changed his name to Louis Gerson and settled in Akron, Ohio, where, working as a fruit wholesaler, he saved enough money to purchase passage for his wife and daughter six years later. Louis became an American citizen in 1928; Esther followed suit in September 1939, twenty days after Hitler's invasion of Poland. They had three more children in the United States, including my father, born in 1930.

The CD traces a Jewish family's integration into American society. There is a shot of the Akron synagogue, on whose steps immigrant families, including the Gersons, proudly posed after services. Photographs of other institutions follow: the local Workmen's Circle, where adults listened to speakers warn about Hitler and kids learned Yiddish; Buchtel High school—Berl wore a crisp white shirt and a pinstripe suit for his senior-year picture in 1948; the Jewish Center day camp, where he worked as a counselor; and the University of Akron, where he was among the tallest of his fraternity brothers, with dark hair, thick eyebrows, and the sparkling smile of a young man who expected only good things. Berl then went off into the world: Fort Benning for his military service in the mid-1950s and then Chicago, where he earned an MBA, began a career as a CPA for a Big Five accounting firm, and wore dark suits and narrow ties.

In 1960, the year he turned thirty, my father accepted a transfer to Brussels. This was his first overseas stay. The photographs now depict a different social world. Here he is with Belgian and expat friends: Britons, Greeks, and Americans who sported ascots while sipping cocktails on the patio of the Tudor-style villa they rented on summer weekends in the swank Flemish resort of Knokke-le-Zoute. Here he is sandwiched between bikini-clad girls in the Israeli port of Eilat, smiling broadly on the Greek island of Corfu, and drinking tall beers on a terrace in Prague. And here he is at sea, greeting the captain of an ocean liner at a black-tie dinner somewhere between New York and Rotterdam, which he may or may not have remembered at the time as his father's port of departure forty-odd years earlier.

The photographs he selected depict a glorious immigrant experience, a tale of familial sacrifice, achievement, and tangible rewards. There was no reference to anti-Semitism; the story was of unimpeded progress. There were no traces either of his wife and children. In his accompanying notes, Berl explained that he was sharing these photographs "so that other family members could enjoy them." Though I appreciated his gesture, I wondered why he had left us out. He had titled the CD "Bernard Gerson—Ancestors to 1964." Belarus and the ancestors seemed to exist only as preambles to a personal success story that ended the year before he met my mother.

Berl wrote "Album 1" on the CD, but when I asked him whether he intended to give us a second one, he said no. There was to be no record of his affectionate embraces and sudden mood swings, no photographs that corresponded to my own experiences. It was my father's life on that CD and not mine, his history more than ours. So much remained unsaid.

Regardless, I told him that we would go to Belarus.

It was a quick trip: two days in Minsk, with its faded Communist murals and colossal governmental buildings; a day in Bobruisk, where rusty apartment complexes tower above wooden houses in bright colors; and a day in Parichi, the small town that had been home to Berl's maternal family. Our main guide and translator was a short, avuncular Jewish woman whose easy cadence drew me in. I followed Vera as she discussed the Pale of Settlement, the devastation of World War II, and the postwar reconstruction of a wrecked country. Far from the New York streets through which I still wandered alone and the upstate woods in which I sank in white powder, I could escape some of the routines of grief. Still, I was only drifting along—a historian oblivious to history.

Julian, now thirteen, had a difficult time as well. He complained about the food, the lack of amenities, the dirt, the poverty. He also clung tight to his childhood, tickling Vera and hurrying us along during historical visits. In Minsk, he insisted that we play Frisbee in a park filled with monuments to the decimated Jewish population. When I hesitated, he said that the dead wouldn't want us to be upset. It had not crossed my mind that, two years after the death of his brother, a journey in search of other dead relatives would prove unsettling to Julian.

Though I walked by Berl's side, I did not pay close attention to his emotional state. I knew that he was not seeking to fill holes in his family history; the documents in his possession told him everything he wanted to know about ancestors who had lived there since the 1850s at the latest. In the travel journal he later shared with us, Berl related ordinary episodes—for instance, our luncheon with our day guide to Parichi. A silver-haired woman in her sixties, Chana lived in a ramshackle house with a white-brick wood oven and a fly-infested toilet that she drained with a bucket of water. The dining and living rooms evoked the Soviet era, with wallpaper, furniture, rugs, and curtains in various gradations of brown. Berl wrote that Chana awoke at dawn to cook with vegetables from her garden. He then listed the dishes she had set before us: cucumbers and tomatoes, radishes, borscht, sour cream, boiled potatoes, meatballs, and stuffed kishke, or intestine.

Berl wrote at particular length about another episode: an encounter with elderly Jewish men in a Bobruisk community center. These men could not tell us anything about our relatives since they had not grown up in this region, but Berl asked them about their lives and they inquired about his. "I explained that I lived very well now and that I started working at twelve years old," he wrote in his journal. "I wanted to convey that hard work was the basis of success for my generation. Most of the men are retired so they lived under Soviet rule. Not much chance to show initiative in those circumstances."

It had been a long road from Bobruisk to Akron to Brussels, but, standing in a house that could not have differed much from the one his forebears had inhabited or surrounded by men who bore a physical resemblance to his parents, Berl could now sense their presence and connect their wholesome values, which he associated with pre-Soviet shtetls, to those of small-town America, which he linked to democracy and capitalism. "Although we didn't learn anything new about my parents, we were able to get a good feel about the way they lived," Berl wrote.

Berl had come to Belarus to commune with his kin and complete his own family story of escape and growth. I was happy for him, and yet at the same time detached from his experience. When he thanked me on the plane home for accompanying him, I smiled, but found it difficult to look him in the eyes. The story he told—about initiative, hard work and its rewards, people shaping their destiny in a just and controllable world—no longer made sense to me. When I began high school, Berl had told me to write my goals for the four years to come. He taught me to break complex tasks into component parts and devise multiyear plans—a foolproof method for moving forward in the world. That had sustained me for a long time. Now, however, this approach seemed foreign, if not bankrupt.

Nor did his story account for Owen. I had watched from the sidelines as Berl resurrected his ancestors without ever mentioning one of his progeny. It is possible that Owen accompanied him on the trip. Perhaps the two of them held hands on the squares of Bobruisk and the dirt roads of Parichi. Berl's silence was so heavy, however, that I could not tell. It also prevented me from noticing much else. Owen's absence from my father's itinerary made him even more present in mine.

At dinner one evening, Vera had asked me if I had other children at home. I hesitated before answering. The thought crossed my mind that Julian, who looked at me fixedly across the table, or Berl, who cast his eyes down, might want me to say that there had never been another child, or that our other child awaited our return. If I remained silent about Owen, we would all be less distraught.

But I only hesitated for a second because, two years after the accident, I sometimes forgot Owen's towering presence, the rhythm of his step, what it was like to parent him every minute of the day. He was becoming a shadow, or a polished and thus diminished version of his real self. The boy I now remembered seemed so much quieter and more eager to please that I sometimes wondered whether such an imposing being could have existed. Owen had of course existed, and Vera had to know.

She sat at the opposite end of the table, which meant that my words had to cut through my father's silence. Berl did not take hold of them as they passed by—he did not even raise his eyes—but they seemed to weigh him down. His shoulders slumped. I felt sadness for him, but less than for Owen, and less than for Julian, who continued to stare at me as I acknowledged the existence of a boy whose voice could not be heard in the land of his ancestors.

And yet, Owen had not been alone in Belarus.

One morning, our driver failed to show up because his wife had given birth to a stillborn baby the previous night. The next day, I learned that the local woman who guided us in Bobruisk had lost a child years earlier. And the day after that, in Parichi's Jewish cemetery, Chana led us to a black marble grave with white lettering and an engraved portrait of a skinny man with cropped hair and thin lips. Though Chana did not speak English, she conveyed that this was her son. He had died of the flu at the age of thirty-one.

Every day we also came upon desecrated graves. Seventy years earlier, Jewish boys and girls were shot or burned alive in these towns. Twenty thousand Jews still lived in Bobruisk when it fell to the Nazis on June 28, 1941. At that time, in Brussels, Zosia had met a former POW named Jules; in Akron, Berl was eleven and posing for pictures on a couch with his brother and parents.

Belarus, however, became what one historian has called "the deadliest place in the world."

The following autumn and winter, Bobruisk was hit by several *Aktions,* or mass killings, culminating with the liquidation of the Jewish ghetto by members of Police Battalion 316 and Einsatzkommando 8, whose task was to murder the Jews of Belarus. On December 19, an SS officer reported that Bobruisk's Jews had made connections with partisans and refused to work or wear badges—standard Nazi justification for their executions. "By carrying out a special action, a total of 5,281 Jews of both sexes were shot. The town of Bobruisk and its nearby area are free of Jews." In Parichi, "a special action was carried out in the course of which 1,031 Jews and Jewesses were shot."

In both towns, we followed the routes that these children, women, and men had taken as they marched to clearings where they were lined up next to massive ditches and murdered, rows of bodies falling atop one another. Chana related that in Parichi, the head rabbi had told the commanding officer that Germany's persecution of Jews would cost it the war. The officer responded by cutting off his tongue. The rabbi staggered on in shock, blood running down his shirt. According to the town's book of remembrance, the Nazis raised children on spears and tossed them into the pits. In 1944, they dug up the corpses, covered them with tar and gasoline, and set them on fire. Today, an obelisk with a marble base and a red star in the center stands near the ditches, along with urns of wartime remains and the number 10,000 in black concrete. Ehrenberg—the family name of Berl's maternal ancestors—is fourth from the bottom on the obelisk.

Berl jotted this last bit of information in his journal. What he could not have known, and what I did not realize until I returned home, is that Belarus's horrors past and present had made the place strangely hospitable to me. Children had long died in these lands; parents had long lost their sons and daughters and continued to do so. The death of one's child, of an eight-year-old even, is as immeasurably sad there as it is elsewhere. But it finds its place within a universe in which stability, control, and justice are not rights or expectations but aspirations, perhaps even delusions. In this universe, bereaved parents are not culpable in crimes against nature or civilization. They do not have to allay the fears of others or their own by huddling in church basements.

When Chana led us to her son's grave, she stood there without speaking, as if a bereaved mother were the most normal being in the world. Her silence felt different from Berl's or even Ginette's. It was so full of emotion, so embedded in the local terrain, and also so light that it floated above the ground, lifting her as high as the young couple whom Marc Chagall once painted above his native Vitebsk, another Belarusian town whose Jewish population all but vanished. I wanted to tell Chana that I, too, had lost a son, but we had no language in which to communicate and I did not want to convey this through a translator, so I just stood with her, and this was enough.

This kind of silence becomes possible when one no longer expects to understand the suffering or avert the violence of the world. There are of course stories of rescue in Belarus. Some local men and women did for Jews what Charles and Annie did for Zosia and Jules. Minsk's Great Patriotic War Museum honors Elena Valendovich, a Christian who sheltered a Jewish girl she found on a doorstep. The girl's mother had left her there and then watched from a distance as the gentile woman took her home. Other local Christians guided Jews to the *Pushcha*, the forest of thick trees and bushes that provided enough cover to hide and perhaps survive. The Communist partisans who made the forest their own have been commemorated as heroes since the war. They fought the Nazis with courage and worked with the Minsk Ghetto underground to hide thousands of Jews in the woods.

The situation in Minsk was unique, however, and even there only a tiny minority survived. Some people anticipated what was bound to follow the German invasion, found the will and strength to take action, and secured the necessary assistance. But in a country in which more than 350,000 Jews perished—the greater part of the Jewish population that had not fled—who could be expected to save loved ones? You could turn to a neighbor or bribe one more guard or set out for the forest a week earlier and still lose a child. This I learned in these badlands.

This is why, after our return, I attached so much importance to another episode on the trip, a walk that the three of us took before lunch at Chana's. We ended up by the Berezina, a wide river with tall grasses and willows sloping over the surface. As I took in the scene—the flow of the current, an islet within swimming distance, three boys fishing by a half-submerged rowboat—I did not imagine people drowning in these waters. Nor did my thoughts take me to the Green, No-Name Island, or the abandoned red dory we had passed on the day of the accident, pinned against a rock in the middle of the river. The three boys did remind me of Owen—his hair had been as short as theirs that summer—but this was not the first thought to cross my mind.

The image that came to me was of Berl's mother swimming on this spot at the age of eight. When I shared it with my father, he mentioned that his mother and her friends would swim naked, boys and girls apart. Long ago, she had told him about this, he said. But he did not say anything until I brought it up that afternoon; he may not even have remembered.

For a long time, I wondered whether I had taken my father to Belarus or whether he had led me there. Then I realized that both were true. I had inched closer to Berl by the Berezina; he had also drawn me in. He must have needed someone nearby, someone who would mention his mother and watch him summon her to his side. This trip was not only about what Berl would see; it was also about others seeing him. Perhaps this was why he had never gone on his own.

Berl, in turn, had brought me to a land in which those who failed to save loved ones did not necessarily live in shame or guilt. They could continue to lead full lives alongside their parents and children, dead and alive. My father and I both needed our sons on this trip, but for different reasons. For Berl, it was about the past. See where I came from, he seemed to say. For me, who had made sure Julian stood with us by the Berezina, it was about the future. See who I can still be.

When Alison looked back on the second year, she said that life had lost its sharp edges. Owen would not return; this was real now, she said. His death was fading behind the veneer of normalcy, something she had expected since the funeral, when her certainty that Owen would in time vanish from the world compounded her desolation. "One day he'll be a speck in Julian's mind," she once said. "The loss will become more important to him than Owen ever was." Two years in, we had become caretakers of Julian's memories, teaching him about a relationship that was slipping from consciousness.

Still, my grief and Alison's remained distinct. While I continued to feel that I had left Owen behind, Alison continued to notice his presence around her. This presence was not truly Owen, Alison said, but it was something. My inertia still frustrated her;

her manic energy still frazzled me. Without deeming her way superior ("perhaps there is something wrong with me," she let out one day), Alison complained that I no longer fought for anything. During one argument, she called me gutless. It was difficult to object, difficult to tell her that such words took me back to the river, and difficult to understand why she would continue to make her life with such a person.

And yet, something imperceptible changed between us after Belarus. One winter afternoon, we took a walk outside Woodstock, on a quiet road that rises up a hilltop and then slides toward a lake. It was a bitter day, with cold wind sweeping down the barren mountains. As soon as I saw the dark water, I thought of Owen of course and so did Alison, though neither of us said anything. We simply agreed to remain by the edge for a few minutes.

Standing in silence, standing together as if bereaved parents were the most normal beings in the world, we felt the immensity of Owen's absence just as every day Alison felt the immensity of Owen's presence—absence and presence necessarily entwined. It was nothing more than this, a quiet moment by the water. But during the months that followed, it gained density alongside others like it, moments during which the only thing to do was to stand still.

Do not feel compelled to say anything to Alison.

Do not ask whether Owen's death was the worst thing in the world.

Do not expect to understand this inscrutable event, soften its edges, or make it your own.

Do not step away when you feel what it is like not to understand.

Do not expect anything more than stopping by a lake with Alison and feeling together what you will never understand.

I had to go off without Alison in order to stand quietly with her upon returning and feel that this was enough. Likewise, I had to discover distant rivers and forests in order to tell Alison about yet another encounter with the Green, one that I had been keeping to myself.

It happened twenty minutes or so after the accident. While searching for Owen, I ran upstream until a bend or perhaps a tributary blocked the way, preventing me from reaching the place in the river where I had last seen him. I stood at the edge, wanting to cross but kept in place by the rapid current. Within minutes, a guide arrived and stepped into the water, his chest cutting a furrow across the broken-up surface. He told me to stay put, which I did because he was a professional and I was not, and also because he still wore his life jacket whereas I had discarded mine. People die all the time while trying to save others.

Still, how could I be sure that I had not been too fearful to make this crossing? How could I know that I would have sacrificed my life for my son if this might have made a difference?

Alison did not question my actions when I told her about this. Nor did she bring up her own decision to remain on the bank when she had arrived at the same bend. This was a separate matter altogether and clearly not a problematic one for her, probably because she had long recognized what I could not grasp until Belarus—that we could have made it across and run between the trees and perhaps even glimpsed Owen on the other side of the river and still been unable to save him.

EIGHTEEN

Julie: *What kind of boat was it?*

Alison stood by the bedroom window, her body barely discernible in the early morning half-light. *Fuck!* Silence, and then in a softer voice, almost a whisper, a confession: "Sometimes I go back to the river."

She moved from the window to the bed, sat next to me, and apologized for bringing up the accident. There are topics that, from the earliest days, each of us tacitly agreed not to spring upon the other. Evoking sadness in general terms, mentioning a difficult moment that had occurred that day—these things were acceptable. But we did not allow ourselves to measure the void of Owen's absence, or wonder out loud whether we would make it, or say things like *my life is finished*. Nor did we drag the other, unprepared, back to the accident. The image of Owen alone in the water was so painful that, from the start, I refrained from imagining it. What happened during those last minutes on Disaster Falls became a dark hole in the recess of my mind.

I did not write about the accident for many months, even though I knew that those memories, too, would eventually fade. I could not figure out what story to tell, or if it was all right to turn Owen's death into a story, or whether I could write about it with the requisite honesty. Words that are indispensable—a testament to those we love—can also prove insufferable. Could I follow Wladyslaw Szlengel, the Warsaw Ghetto poet who penned such fierce, unsparing verses about unimaginable terror? "The hot steam will begin to suffocate you, to suffocate you, / And you will scream, you will try to run." Shun metaphors, avoid innuendo, refuse flowery language. Cut close to the bone, as close as possible to the substance of things.

Once I finally sat down to write what I could remember about the day's events on the Green—sometime after returning from Belarus—I began with the lead-up to the accident and its aftermath before moving to the history of the rapids. All of this drew me closer, but still not to the heart of the matter.

When there was nothing left but the accident itself, I wrote about that as well. I did so slowly and meticulously, as if granular precision could counterbalance the blur of my grief and allow me to touch that time and place without trembling. Only then did I realize that I had been living every day with what Alison and I did not see and then did not let ourselves imagine: Owen at the moment of his death.

We arrived at Disaster Falls in the middle of the afternoon, after running the Class I rapids that had alarmed and delighted Owen. Before entering this stretch of the river, the lead raft directed us to the left bank, where we dragged our vessels onto the sand and then walked up a short hill. From that height, we would scout the rapids.

All of us walked in single file, up the narrow path. The bottleneck resembled a rapid except that, on land, constriction slows things down, whereas in water it creates turbulence. By the time the four of us reached the top, a crowd had formed around

Delma, who was talking. Maybe she had only cleared her throat; maybe she had told a joke; or maybe she had provided a warning that some of us would not hear. I have no idea, but when I later tried to establish when things first went awry, this is where I ended up.

After the scouting, Alison and Julian would reembark on rafts that guides would pilot. I was slated to run Disaster Falls with Owen in a ducky—not the same thing. During our initial get-together the previous evening in Vernal, Delma had asked who would want to use a ducky at some point on the trip. Many hands went up, though no one asked on what sections of the river we would use duckies or how, in terms of stability and maneuverability, they compared to rafts. This might have been because the outfitters' brochure had already provided answers. It said that duckies were easy to handle in low- or mid-intensity rapids, even for beginners. Riding in a ducky would, it promised, provide a sense of what it was like to be a river otter. There were half a dozen kids eight and above on the trip. All of them would no doubt have loved to become otters for a day.

When we reached the lookout point, I knew that I had to hear Delma's instructions. As I made my way to the front of the group, I gained a clearer view of the river. It stretched out for a few hundred feet before contracting into a channel framed by two large boulders, one on each side. The boulders heralded a drop into rushing waters. This was Upper Disaster. Afterward, the rapids slowed down, with no more drops, although the water soon gathered speed as it circled and slammed into rocks of all sizes, including the largest one—No-Name Island, which bifurcated the river. This went on for a quarter of a mile, into Lower Disaster.

———

Delma presented the initial gauntlet, framed by the boulders, as the greatest challenge. She told us to enter the rapids straight on and to follow the raft that preceded us. Upon reaching the calmer stretch below, we were to hang left and make our way to an eddy, where the party would regroup. While focus was required throughout, things would grow easier past the gauntlet. My gut feeling, however, was that nothing about Disaster Falls would be easy. The margin of error seemed slim on rapids that had little in common with the morning's Class I's. They represented an exponential shift, a portal into a different realm. I felt this on the lookout point even though the magnitude of the shift and the precise nature of this realm eluded me.

Something did not feel right, but I could not be sure. The brochure had presented Upper Disaster as a Class III, ideal for children. Some of the guidebooks I later consulted agree, but not all. William McGinnis's *Whitewater Rafting* says that Upper and Lower Disaster are rated Class IV and II in low water. The *River Runner's Guide to Utah* labels the entire Gates of Lodore section of the Green *advanced*, meaning that it requires "fast maneuvers under pressure" and may make self-recovery difficult. The book recommends training on the type of kayak or canoe one will use. "How rough are Dinosaur's rapids?" asks *Belknap's Waterproof Dinosaur River Guide.* Not as difficult as the Grand Canyon's heavy water, but "tricky enough to challenge veteran river runners."

One of the many things I did not know during the scouting was that experienced kayakers have spent considerable time on that spot, preparing to run the rapids in vessels not dissimilar to mine except that they were nimble, one-person, hard-shell kayaks rather than unwieldy two-person duckies with a child in the front.

The environmentalist Jeffrey St. Clair and his party once

scouted Disaster Falls for an hour, considering rocks and boulders that waited to "trap a foot, rip a raft, smash a skull." Colin Fletcher, the backpacker, once stood for a long time where I now stood, scoping possible routes. *If you ferried left down the smooth tongue above the rapid and established momentum toward the far bank, a few fierce strokes at the proper moment should take you beyond the boulder that formed the left flank of the chute and into a small, relatively slack patch of water. From there, an apparently easy route bypassed the main drop. Below, a short stretch of water without major obstacles would give you time to set up for the rapid's second part.*

Fletcher then walked a short distance to scout the rest of Upper Disaster. *Its main channel ran for perhaps three hundred yards, right of No Name Island, in an almost straight line. But it ran broken and confused.*

After stopping for lunch, Fletcher looked some more and re-read parts of a book entitled *River Rescue*, which warned about places in the river where "the undertow could suck you and pin you there, helpless, until you drowned." He then awaited the arrival of another party to ask their opinion and call on them if needed during his run. Only at that point did he feel ready.

Enter right of center, try to ease left until winging close to the island; then, just beyond a big angular boulder, move back center for a clear final run to the tail.

St. Clair and Fletcher went ahead, but others did not. One blogger I came across scouted this stretch of the river and then deemed it more prudent to run the rapids in a raft instead. We had never anticipated that Owen would run Disaster Falls or any other Class III rapids in a ducky or a kayak. It just so happened that Julian had boarded the ducky in the morning while Owen did so in the afternoon, until we reached Disaster Falls.

Now we had to decide. Owen could stay in the ducky, or he could board a raft.

As people milled about and began walking back to the beach, I took a few steps toward the edge. It was difficult to analyze the situation without rafting experience, training, or prior knowledge of these rapids. Yet the flow of the current, the sound of the water, the droplets in the air made Disaster Falls feel as formidable as it must have in the 1860s. Its name no longer seemed a relic, a metaphor, or a marketing gimmick. I thought about the red dory pinned against a rock. The force of the current had stalled efforts to dislodge it for more than two weeks.

But there was such bonhomie within the party. The first rapids had been so much fun. Our friends had had such a good time on this same stretch of the river a year earlier. And these were *duckies* everyone was talking about—duckies on a river named after a color, duckies in a national monument called Dinosaur.

As I write this, I cannot tell whether I am transcribing what went through my mind on that hill or telling a story I composed during the years that followed. What is certain is that Alison and I talked it over on the point and decided to ask the guides whether it was safe for an inexperienced boater to kayak Disaster Falls with an eight-year-old.

I caught sight of Kris and took him aside. After listening to me and asking about Owen's swimming abilities, he said we could safely run Disaster Falls in a ducky. It would be fine, he said, and then he walked away, leaving me with the rapids at my back and before me a human current sweeping down the hill toward the river. Kris had not stammered or hesitated. There was no reason to question the judgment of a guide who spoke with such authority.

And yet, I still harbored doubts. So I found Delma and took her aside. After listening to me, she, too, said Owen and I could safely run Disaster Falls in our ducky. It would be fine, she said, and then she walked away. She spoke with as much authority as Kris, without stammering or hesitating.

It felt as if we had entered a world in which everything pointed in one direction only. The guides' separate yet identical recommendations, their expertise and assurances, the collective expectations of the group gathered force until running Disaster Falls in a ducky with Owen seemed not only permissible, but perfectly reasonable.

We still had to decide.

Owen and Julian had, like Alison and me, listened to Delma's instructions while viewing the rapids. Now they were part of our conversation, which veered between unarticulated forebodings and the assumption that everything was under control. Owen dithered; Julian offered to switch places with him; and then Owen no longer hesitated. He now insisted upon running the rapids with me in the ducky.

At Arches National Park a few days earlier, Alison and I had told Owen that it was too dangerous to make that steep run down to Delicate Arch. We could have overridden the guides and done the same at Disaster Falls by telling Owen that he would have to ride in a raft. But we could not say no every time and still instill confidence and prepare him for what life had in store. Saying no would tell Owen to choose a safe and protected existence over an exposed and passionate one. Saying no would deprive him of the freedom for which, at his age, I had yearned. Saying no would allow my cautious, protective nature to rule yet again. Saying no would stifle Owen on what he called the best day of his life.

Still, we came so very close to saying no at Disaster Falls.

In the early months after the accident, Alison sometimes wondered whether she had approached life with too much nonchalance. In her Regret.O.Gram (part of a project in which people were invited to pen missives of atonement for Yom Kippur), she apologized to Owen for allowing him to push the limits on that day. Alison kept guilt at bay, however, by repeating what she had first said in the tent: revisiting the past would do no good. Alison never brought up the scouting.

My approach was different. I reviewed this sequence of events from multiple perspectives to understand why we had ultimately said yes. Surely there were reasons for this.

I began with the notion (which I had read somewhere) that people usually make smart decisions when given good information, but often struggle to secure such information from experts. The guides had answered the question I had posed, but not the ones I had failed to ask, such as: What was the probability of flipping over on this rapid—in a ducky as well as in a raft? What was this probability for novices? And what would flipping entail in this current? I wondered if the guides had known. It was difficult to consider this without succumbing to anger, so I told myself that if such information was available, I had not known how to draw it out.

I also reconsidered my upbringing within a social group—the middle class—that believes in its ability to master uncertainty and nature because it is convinced that life will always keep improving, that risk can be reduced or even eliminated, and that days will follow one another without unforeseen disasters. An essay by the critic William Deresiewicz seemed to capture my unwitting assumptions before the accident: "We're going to live a long time, and the world is not going to take us by surprise." There are other ways of thinking about the middle class, but this one resonated. I grew up in the 1970s and 1980s, an era of unprecedented peace in the West. To be sure, Soviet missiles were frightening to anyone living in Belgium during those decades. But the Berlin Wall came down just as I graduated from college. Why not believe in the end of history and a right to happiness, or at the very least *my* right to happiness? Down deep, I must have felt that things would always turn out fine. I certainly did not approach the guides—agents of an ostensibly benevolent corporation—with the fine-honed skepticism of people whose life experiences had taught them how dangerous such trust could be.

These explanations, though persuasive, did not suffice. After the accident, I also lived with questions, such as, How did we come through 9/11 and then lose Owen after all? I lived with the reductive yet powerful notion that Owen was a casualty of our self-indulgent quest for a wilderness experience that has long been commercialized for tourists. I lived with Julian's statement, uttered in passing a couple of years after the accident, that I should have listened to my instincts. I lived with the conviction that, after child molesters perhaps, delinquent parents are the worst sinners in our society.

Yet I also lived with gratitude: Alison and I had made this decision together, and for this, perhaps perversely, I was thankful.

Although we made the decision together, we did not make it alone: Owen participated in the process as well. Owen died as a child—too small to battle those elements—but he was until the end an autonomous being, determined to overcome his anxieties and fashion his own sense of self. Things did not merely happen *to* Owen at Disaster Falls. As much as we manage our children's lives, they also shape their own destinies. This jumped at me when I finally wrote about the scouting, although it took me awhile to make peace with the notion that my child was in any way involved in his own death.

Alison and the boys took their time walking down the hill. Owen and Julian joked about what would happen if one of them died. Who would get the PlayStation? I could not hear them because I hurried down to the water. Julian told me about this banter years later. He cherished this last memory of Owen— laughing with his brother.

By the river, travelers were taking sips from canteens and applying sunscreen while the guides pulled the heavy rafts toward the water. I walked over to the edge and crouched next to our ducky. Invisible to the others or perhaps all too noticeable, I stared at the rapids with enough intensity to etch their course into my brain and muscles. Then, still crouching, I shut my eyes.

The air was still but heavy with the rumble of the river. Without leaving the shoreline, I descended Disaster Falls, or rather Owen and I ran Disaster Falls, straight down the middle, between the boulders, and then sharply to the left, far from the rocks we could see and the others that lurked below the surface.

Colin Fletcher had once stood there and traced his own itinerary. An expert outdoorsman, he knew just how tentative his plan had to be. *A mere expression of intent. I'd have to feel my way down, making moment-to-moment decisions, obstacle to obstacle.*

My gut told me the same thing, but all I could summon was the advice in the outfitter's brochure: relax and let nature take over.

NINETEEN

Kara: *Were there rocks beneath you?*

The gauntlet went fine; the gauntlet was mayhem.

We proceeded in a line, rafts up front and duckies in the rear. I paddled with purpose from the moment we left the beach, eyes locked on the center point between the boulders. This is exactly where I entered Upper Disaster. The current propelled us over the chute, an abrupt but smooth dip—first the bow carrying Owen, at a fifty-degree angle, and then the stern. Balance seemed more important than skill or agility. After all that mental preparation, we were on the other side of the drop within a fraction of a second.

The rafts continued toward Lower Disaster except for two of them, which the guides stationed on opposite sides of the river. Julian and a guide sat in one near the right bank; Alison and Kris were in the other. Alison chatted with Kris—he told her about Powell's expedition—and snapped what turned out to be the last photograph of Owen. It is all grays and browns and greens: water, rocks, trees. In the center, a shiny yellow ducky carries two blurry yet erect figures with yellow helmets. I am thrusting my paddle into the water, but Owen is holding his horizontally. Though I had asked him to help out, he was not open to instruction right then. He was eight years old.

In that photograph, we are passing a boulder twice our size, with two others like it in the background and more ahead, along with several smaller jagged rocks. The photograph does not capture the strength of the current except around the rocks, where the frothy water rises unevenly. Owen appears to be taking in the scene. I cannot tell whether he is grabbing his paddle for support, like a ballet barre, or clutching it with glee, like a roller-coaster lap bar. Either way, he seems small.

Alison took this picture as we glided along the surface. We had made it past the main obstacle, and for a fleeting instant it felt as if we were hanging above the water. Without saying anything, Owen and I shared the moment like two warriors reliving a glorious victory.

It is at this exact instant that things fell apart. It began behind us, as the other duckies went over the drop. I heard a commotion, loud voices, and the sound of a whistle. An eleven-year-old boy had fallen out of the ducky in which he rode with his father. Kris yelled, "Swimmer!" All eyes were on the kid as he climbed back in. Meanwhile, a teenage girl lost her paddle in the rapids and somehow made it to Alison's raft for assistance. Soon there was another boater in the water. It was either the traveler from San Francisco or his friend. One of them, kayaking solo, had capsized.

I turned around and saw this swimmer not far behind. Since no one else was close, I thought I should help him out. But the guide in Julian's raft shouted commands from his side of the river. I resumed my course.

Bad things could happen anywhere on Upper Disaster, not just on the gauntlet. Colin Fletcher was scanning downstream for obstacles when one of his oars hit bottom in the murky water and jammed so tight that it slipped out. Fletcher dipped his hand in the water and, almost miraculously, recovered the oar. Another kayaker I read about ran into more serious trouble. One of his oars snapped as he approached a big midstream rock. To avoid a wrap, he oriented his bow toward the obstacle and, when he got close, used his other oar to push the kayak away. Afterward, he felt fortunate to have made it out of Disaster Falls.

I veered left, toward the channel that would take us to the eddy and our rendezvous point. But in the midst of this commotion—swimmers in the water, oars floating away, guides yelling from their rafts—the current had drawn us toward the right bank. Fractions of a second, the slightest of distractions: that's all it took, a minute change in location with immediate consequences.

We were now heading for a large boulder. It was my turn to make moment-to-moment decisions. I paddled hard and told Owen to do the same. He followed my instructions, but he was not strong and even if he had been, there is little we could have done against the current.

We hit the boulder head on. This was better than sideways, even though the rapids lapped at our ducky from all directions. I pushed against the boulder with my paddle, a few quick thrusts that got us back on course.

Owen and I continued to paddle. We had entered a treacherous zone, peppered with rocks of all dimensions. Another boulder stood in our path, the same size as the first but only a few feet away, leaving no time to prepare. We hit it at an angle, which made it impossible to dislodge before the current pushed the stern forward and left us perpendicular to the flow.

Owen and I had wrapped around a rock just below Upper Disaster.

One of the bloggers I later read, an Englishwoman living in California, ran Disaster without a hitch, but saw one of her friends flip in the rapids. The ducky was pinned against a huge rock, and then someone came to the woman's help. All of them, the blogger wrote, now understood "the value of having our safety kayaker, Brian, along for the ride."

On her raft, Alison realized that we were stuck. She told Kris, who was still tending to the girl who had lost her paddle. Kris yelled out to the guide who sat in Julian's raft, across the river. Alison does not remember what Kris said.

Afterward, things unfolded like this: fast, then slow, then fast.

Fast. Water swarmed in, first a series of wavelets and then a steady flow that filled up one end of the ducky and pushed it against a rock that provided no traction whatsoever. Alison and Julian both saw the ducky shoot straight up, with the bow toward the skies and Owen hanging above the river.

Things happened quickly, a violent passage from one state to another, all faculties summoned to process the new reality. The images I carry are spotty and out of focus: water, stones inches away, the ducky twisting to its side, lost paddles. No sound.

Julian recognized the purple water bottle clipped to our bow. The bottle, too, was up in the air.

Two more swimmers.

When Alison told Kris that this was a lot, she heard him say that it was the most he had ever seen or else the most he had seen in a while—one of the two. Alison felt her stomach tighten.

If someone blew a whistle, I could not hear it because I was underwater.

Slow. As soon as my life jacket pulled me to the surface, I saw Owen in the water. He was facing me, between ten and fifteen feet away. The ducky must have done a 180 because we had switched positions.

He was now upstream, his back to the gauntlet, his face toward the rocks and Lower Disaster and the flow of a river that had many miles to go before meeting the Colorado. I was now downstream, with Julian to my left and, behind Owen, the traveler from San Francisco or his friend climbing into a ducky. All I could see was Owen's face against the water, a white and yellow buoy on a green river.

It was just the two of us, close and out of reach. I had been unable to grab Owen when the ducky twisted and could not do so now either. Over the years, I had taken his hand in subway stations and atop canyons, but at this moment we could not touch each other, not even if we stretched our arms. Worlds can come undone in infinitesimal increments.

Owen and I were suspended in the water, his eyes locked on mine and mine on his. The force of the current was bearing down on his back and my chest. Everything was already in motion, nature and history reasserting their rights with impatience. Still, we remained in place, our gazes denying the past of Disaster Falls while keeping the future at bay.

When I peered into Owen's eyes, I did not see fear or anguish. Owen did not panic. He did not open his mouth or flail his arms or blink any more than usual. He was concerned, he seemed to grasp the seriousness of the situation, but his eyes remained steady, assessing his circumstances and weighing options. He appeared to know that everything had changed and that he would have to find his way on his own. Later I would wonder what he had seen in my eyes, and also whether I had conjured up a soothing image of Owen—the only image I could bear. If I did manufacture such an image, then I did so right there in the water, when time stood still for an eternity that could not have lasted more than a second.

I could say only one thing within that split second, which meant that I had no time to think about what it would be. I told Owen to keep his feet above water—something I remembered from the morning's safety meeting. The guide had taught us what to do in case we flipped, which was presented as an unlikely possibility. Raise your hands if you need help, tap your helmet if everything is fine. Most important, turn your body so that it faces downriver, and keep your feet elevated to avoid entrapment around underwater rocks. You don't want to end up in a strainer sieve, an opening between trees or rocks that lets water through but collects branches and bodies.

I do not remember raising my hands in the rapids while facing Owen, but this may be what he saw as I urged him to keep his feet above water. I said this as loudly as I could, with the stern intensity of the parent who senses but does not yet know, or cannot yet admit, that he is losing control over his child's fate.

Keep your feet above water: These words had to be said, but they now seem so prosaic, so mundane. This continues to make me sad. I wish that my last exchange with Owen had entailed something besides advice.

Fast. The rapids drew me under. I tried to keep my feet up but could not even raise my head above the surface. The river was flipping me like a twig, propelling me from one submerged rock to another, flesh and bone crashing into inanimate matter. Eventually I repositioned myself in a semi-seated position that made it possible to kick off the boulders. But the effort and the lack of oxygen exhausted me.

I thought that I might die. This, I now know, was no outlandish notion. A few years earlier, a father and child had capsized in Class III rapids down the river. The child survived, but the father drowned after his foot became trapped. The possibility of dying filled me with disbelief: Death in these circumstances? Why are we even here?

And if I am about to die, then what is happening to Owen?

The rapids suddenly let up and dumped me into the eddy below No-Name Island. I swam to the closest raft, Delma's, and asked if she had seen Owen. She had not; nobody had. Julian and his guide joined us within minutes. They had picked up our ducky but had lost sight of Owen after the accident. Kris and Alison never saw him either. As they made their way down the river, Alison had peered into every raft, hoping to find in one of them the boy who had vanished during the confusion at Upper Disaster.

———

Owen's body was found hours later near the right bank, in a sieve. He was still wearing his helmet and safety jacket. In the tent, Alison deemed this recovery a blessing. Otherwise, she said, it would have been a search without end, countless days on the river, lingering uncertainty about Owen's life or death.

We will never know what exactly happened to Owen. On some days, I remembered him as strong and tenacious and told myself that he died in the throes of a valiant battle. At the very least, he was doing something he loved, like the high-wire artist Philippe Petit, the man who walked between the Twin Towers and once said that if he were to fall, what a beautiful thing it would be to die in the exercise of his passion. On those days, I pictured Owen's face on the river and saw equanimity.

Such thoughts did not come easily. Owen's could not be a beautiful death. But I listened intently when Alison's mother and her partner confided that, a year before the accident, Owen had told them something he had never shared at home. He had said that even though he looked like other children, he could see things they could not. Shortly thereafter, a family friend disclosed that Owen had told her about a benevolent force that always accompanied him. He saw it from a corner of his eye. Because Owen knew that our friend had worked as an ER technician, he asked her what happened to people when they died. He was especially curious about near-death experiences and survivors of prolonged comas.

Our friend said that Owen talked about such matters without apprehension. This made me think of one of my favorite photographs of Owen and Julian: a three-quarter shot taken in a park when they were six and nine. Julian smiles, mouth half-open, eyes darting to his left. He is fully immersed in childhood. Owen's cheek almost touches his, but he does not lean on his brother and there is nothing childlike about him. His mouth is shut, without a smile; his eyes are melancholy yet focused. He is staring at the camera, into the camera, past the camera, as if he had discerned a secret expanse across some distant horizon.

Our friend expressed the hope that her talks with Owen had brought him some comfort on the river. "Perhaps he understood . . ." She did not finish her sentence, but if Owen could see things that we could not, if he was never alone after all, then it was possible that he had forged a connection of his own with the broader world, a connection that made his dying something more than stark, definitive agony. Maybe Owen had some acquaintance with death, maybe it was less foreign to him. I had not spent enough time out West to imagine Owen as some version of the rugged frontiersman who, as Theodore Roosevelt once put it, faces death "as he has faced many other evils, with quiet, uncomplaining fortitude." But after that conversation I allowed myself to believe that Disaster Falls had not caught him by surprise.

Owen had disclosed other things in his conversations with my mother-in-law, her partner, and our family friend. He had also said that strange thoughts went through his mind and that he sometimes saw red flashes and odd shapes on the carpet and walls. He could not stop such thoughts.

Alison and I had never known about this or considered that, as he posed next to Julian in that photograph, Owen saw something that unsettled him, something he could not escape. Maybe he struggled to fall asleep at night because he was confronting these flashes and shapes along with the prospect of final solitude.

This yielded a different mental image of the accident, one

that for a long time I never put into words. But whenever I now heard a child cough up water or saw a father throw his son into the air, my chest tightened and my breathing accelerated just as Owen's must have on the river, when his fear of abandonment became reality and he found himself alone in the water. Unless I removed myself, I ended up in the sieve with him, both of us pinned against a rock, like the red dory whose name we had made out as we passed by earlier that day. *The Great Unknown*, it was called.

This is the point of no return, filled with thoughts that, like a serrated knife, scrape the inner lining of the skin. When we visited Owen's school, some of his classmates asked how long he had spent underwater and what he looked like. I could not answer because I had not wanted to know. I did read in a dentist's waiting room that drowning occurs when water destroys a thin membrane in the lungs. It is remarkably easy for this membrane to stop functioning; a gulp or two can suffice. Julian blurted out as much one day. Drowning is not that bad, he told me: some pain at the outset and then a rapid feeling of euphoria. He had read this online.

Regardless, Owen had been pulled under. Perhaps I simply needed the image of his serene face to counter my own fear of death.

Alison did not carry such images. She also said that her view of death changed after the accident. She did not look forward to dying, but she did not dread it either. What had been everlasting nothingness became a respite from emptiness and a reunion with Owen. I could not help but think once again of our different experiences on the river. Alison had not veered off course in a ducky, she had not seen Owen's face in the water, she had not been sucked under. Our loss was the same but not its circumstances. This must have explained other things as well:

Alison never wished that, on the bus ride to the boat launch, she had read *River Rescue* rather than a collection of short stories about New York City.

Alison never checked the National Water Information System for the Green River's real-time water flow on the day of the accident.

Alison never had dreams in which she caught Owen as he slipped from a ladder.

Alison never walked along the Hudson and imagined that, should a child fall into the river, she would dive in before anyone else. She never wished for this to happen, and never vowed to keep this unspeakable thought to herself.

Alison never stopped swimming. Soon after the accident, I watched her jump back into pools. Undulating like a seal, she glided along the walls and delved into corners before coming up for air. Alison said that she had learned this from Owen. Sometimes she swam underwater until her lungs emptied out and began to burn. She did it to feel Owen's presence, to reach that place that neither one of us could avoid.

There is one other thing Alison never did: ask me how I could have allowed this to happen. She could have inquired openly or discreetly, through an inflection in her voice, a glance, a gesture. Without uttering a word, she could have told me I had lost her child.

I remained on the lookout for subtle assignations of blame but detected nothing. When I thanked her for forgiving me, she replied that she had nothing to forgive because I had not done anything wrong. There was something ethereal about the grace Alison displayed and the grace she bestowed. Our therapist said that she had never before counseled a couple in which the spouse less directly involved did not blame the other. Alison had given me a gift I could never repay.

We both agreed that if our roles had been reversed that afternoon, things would probably have proven more complicated afterward. I believed in causes and effects and responsibility and hence blame. Alison did not, at least not within the family, which means that she did not blame herself either. Though she asked me if we had screwed up, she never revisited our decisions to book the trip or allow Owen on the rapids. She never reexamined what she had said or refrained from saying during the scouting. "It is not about us, only about Owen," Alison explained.

Perhaps there was nothing to revisit. But while Alison's attitude felt liberating, it also struck me as inexplicable. Surely blame had lodged itself somewhere within her psyche. Maybe this is why she had apologized after bringing us back to the river that morning in the bedroom. She may have sensed that something could slip out.

Alison's unwillingness to blame did not mean that our world was without blame. Surely someone bore responsibility. The blame thus fell upon me and, more often than not, it ended with me—the scouting, the ducky, the rapids. There was a churned-up demon inside my body, something I felt with sharpened intensity during each physical breakdown. Had Alison assigned blame and perhaps taken some blame—even a little—our marriage might have collapsed. But if we named and shared the blame, then I might not have reexamined the circumstances of the accident as often as I did, questioning our decisions, the events that played out on the river, and the story I preferred to ignore, the one about people who make bad calls because they only hear what they want to hear.

Had Alison assigned blame, I might not have told her, as I did one day, that I wished that, on the lookout point, she had urged me to run Disaster Falls in a raft instead of a ducky. And she might not have told me that same day and only that one time what I needed to hear in someone else's voice: namely, that she wished that I had been stronger and faster, more decisive and assertive that day on the Green.

TWENTY

Sarah: *I know how it feels to lose someone
because I lost my grandmother.*

Four months after Belarus, on a Sunday afternoon, my mother called from Brussels with a shaky voice. Berl had ferocious stomach pain. They were awaiting test results, but she was not hopeful.

"It's very bad," she said.

My mother could not tell what my father felt or sensed at that point but when they drove to the doctor's office three days later, he warned her not to expect good news, and when they walked out, he put his head on her shoulder and kissed her cheek, something he did only rarely.

One of my great-aunts had died of pancreatic cancer when I was a child: we knew what the words meant. My thoughts went first to my father's death rather than the ordeal to come or the tumor that had been growing inside his body, even in Belarus. Owen had died in a blur, leaving no time to say anything. Afterward, time seemed to freeze: Owen always eight, always entering fourth grade, always looking into my eyes in the middle of a river. Within weeks, the machinery of time began to creak, slowly at first and then faster with each revolution. The acceleration proved nearly indiscernible—something you feel before you see—but it sucked up memories while leaving Owen behind.

This would be different. Berl's death would stretch out until he reached the faint light we could already make out on the horizon. There would be time to track the smallest shifts and anticipate new stages in the disease, time for Berl to die and for us to watch him die.

I did not expect to cry with Berl, whose silence in Belarus still weighed heavily on me. But perhaps I could sit with him and talk about things that had happened long before the accident and afterward as well. Or perhaps things would go differently now that he had entered a phase of life that did not fit on his CD. Perhaps my father would sit by my side and say things that had not been said before.

I knew too little about cancer to manage my expectations. After my mother's phone call, I went to the Hudson to be with Berl. Since the accident, I had wondered whether any loss would ever compare to Owen's, whether I would even be able to properly mourn my parents when the time came. Now I wondered how to continue grieving for my son while remaining present for my father. But along the river, all I could find were traces of Owen. There did not seem to be room for anyone else.

A few days later, my mother met Alison and me at the Brussels airport and drove us to the hospital, where Berl was being treated for an infection. He was sitting up in bed, waiting for us. My mother pulled up a chair near him; Alison and I sat across from them, on the other bed in the room.

Though my father spoke in a firm voice, his face was pale, and he asked my mother to rub his sore shoulder. As her fingers massaged his parched skin, digging into muscles that I remembered as so much firmer, Alison lay back and fell asleep. She had insisted upon making the trip even though she had found it difficult to leave Julian alone. Back in New York, she had winced while hearing me speak to my sister, who lived in Seattle, about care options for my father. This conjured up a future in which Julian was left to confront our end-of-life travails on his own. Owen's death and my father's were entwined around the prospect of our own passing and Julian's solitude in the world.

We remained in that hospital room for much of the afternoon. Berl talked about his symptoms and what lay ahead. He said things like "Let's take it one day at a time." This pragmatic approach, which broke time down into manageable parcels, had served him well over the years. It told me that things do not always change irrevocably the moment one enters the realm of the ill, the wounded, the dying. Even as his body broke down, Berl might remain steady, he might remain himself.

But his body would break down, and this expectation brought me back to the first months after the accident, when people looked to Alison and me for guidance. Though Berl did not ask for advice, I told him that people would not come to him if he appeared closed in or helpless; they would not know how to do so. You have to guide them, I said. You have to provide a way in.

My father was discharged in the evening. The four of us spent the weekend in my parents' apartment, which felt as low and gray as the Belgian sky. We ate, and talked a little, and looked out the windows as rain fell on the small garden that Berl had tended for years. Before dinner on Saturday, he invited me into his office to go over his assets and talk about estate taxes. Our conversation ended with burial plans. Cremation had long been his preference, but he now told me that a cemetery funeral might be best for the family. When I looked into his eyes, I saw resolve and lucidity. I muttered that he seemed to be holding up. "I don't express all that's going on inside," he said.

My mother had no difficulty expressing what was going on inside her. As I walked out of my bedroom early Sunday morning, she stopped me in the dark hallway. I expected her to say something about my father, but she apologized instead for her inability to help after Owen's death. She had not found a way of making herself available, she said, and this continued to fill her with guilt. "Do you feel guilty?" she asked before adding that I should not. We never spoke about this again—her guilt and mine—although at some point that weekend I mentioned Disaster Falls and my mother gasped. Until that moment I had never told my parents the name of the rapids.

Alison and I packed our bags after breakfast. My father had always been the one to drive us to the airport, but this time he bade us good-bye at the front door. He hugged us both, first Alison and then me. As he relaxed his embrace, I thought I saw tears in his eyes. I could not be certain, but during the ride to the airport I wished that I had held him tighter and longer.

While Berl lost muscle strength and felt discomfort during the early months, he could still manage daily activities. He said it had taken him two weeks to get past the shock. Once you accept the reality, he added, you just get on with life without thinking too much about the disease. I felt relieved yet mystified. He now acted as if he would live a long time. When the new year approached, he asked my mother to buy him a calendar, and when the chemo's side effects let up for a day or two, he hailed it as progress. My father held on to the framework around which he had built his entire existence. Until the last month of his life, he told my mother that he was not as sick as she claimed. It was as if the conversation he and I had had about his will and cremation had never taken place.

My mother never heard him ask his oncologist a single question, let alone request a prognosis. But the day after he died, I noticed a book on his bedside table: a memoir by a journalist who had survived two bouts of cancer. Berl's bookmark remained where he had left it. Leafing through the early chapters, I realized that he must have read the passage on page 33 in which a doctor found a tumor near the author's pancreas. The author wrote that if this turned out to be cancer rather than a tumor resting on the organ, "the chances of my survival . . . would have been even slimmer than they were."

"Your father knew," my mother said when I told her about this. "He was a smart man. My aunt died of pancreatic cancer. He knew."

One could see the disease gnawing at him. Each month brought new symptoms: decreased appetite, weight loss, an inflated belly. There were habits and pastimes he abandoned because he no longer cared or forgot: glucosamine supplements, flossing, Sudoku, *Curb Your Enthusiasm*. Fastidious in the past, he now left half-eaten bowls of yogurt throughout the apartment. Berl continued to ask me about my life, but less often. When I walked into his room four months after the diagnosis and found him sleeping with his hands clenched on his stomach, his face the color of chalk, I moved close to make sure he was breathing. This, I told myself, was the face he saw in the mirror—if he still looked.

Berl had always been a bit of a hypochondriac. Every fever might prove fatal; blood pressure had to be measured daily. He said he loved life so much that he did not want to die. Alison now remarked that Berl feared dying alone whereas my mother feared living alone.

Each time I flew to Brussels during those months, I expected a far-reaching, transformative conversation. On one occasion, Berl alluded to a bad day—something that seemed to involve peering into the abyss, imagining the world without him. The rest of the time he sat without speaking in the living room. We both did, side by side. We read, we watched TV, we hid behind laptop screens.

"The silence is the worst," my mother said. In return for her care, she wanted to talk about their marriage and what he was now going through and what would happen to her once he was gone. She was angry, but I felt disappointed and sad, not only for him, but also for this lost opportunity to bridge the distance between us.

If Berl was grieving his own death, he did so within a silence so deep that no one dared breach it. And yet death permeated the apartment—the imminence of death, the energy expended to battle the idea of death, to refute the very possibility. I found it impossible to spend any amount of time with Berl without confronting my own mortality alongside his.

I wondered how I would handle illness when it struck, how I would face my last days. I had hoped that Owen's death might alter my outlook on death, but my bodily breakdowns after the accident had only sharpened my fear. For me, death remained a void, nothingness, the end of it all, pure absence. I felt guilty about this, too—guilty for not changing enough and for expecting too much of my father. I had led the way after Owen's death but now looked to him for direction.

Around this time, Julian voiced trepidation of his own about death. After the accident, he had found comfort in listening to people talk about Owen. This told him that, although his brother had died, he was not entirely gone. Two years later, people had grown quiet and Owen seemed so far away. The stillness of the night allowed dark thoughts (as Julian called them) to colonize his mind. He postponed going to sleep and sometimes asked us to sit with him in bed. I wanted to tell him what I had said to Owen when he had asked about death at the age of six or seven, namely that he was so young and had a long life to live. But I could neither utter such words nor tell Julian that I did not dread death. There was nothing to do, really, except to concede that his dark thoughts were mine as well.

Though Berl had not brought up his own death since the day we planned his funeral, I expected him to say something about Owen's, or at least mention his name, which is why I dropped references in the hope that he would seize upon one of them. All I heard was his new mantra: "I've had eighty good years and one bad one."

I nodded when he uttered these words, which seemed to soothe him, but if he had had eighty good years, where did that leave the two years that separated the accident from his diagnosis? Where did that leave Owen?

On my third visit to Brussels, eight months after the first one, Berl asked me to water the flowers with him. As a child, I had been expected to serve as his helper in the yard, a chore I despised, and we had not gardened together since. But he could no longer do it on his own. His bloated legs provided little support; he had already fallen several times.

I uncoiled the hose and fed it to him as he walked gingerly across the narrow lawn, from one bed to another. I kept my eye on him except for a few seconds, when I kneeled down to untangle the hose. Almost immediately, I heard my father call my name—a plaintive, urgent summons. He had lost his balance on the steps that led from the lawn to the patio. Looking up, I saw him falling backward, hanging in midair, arms spread out, time suspended once again. I lunged and caught him before he hit the ground. His frail body, a sack of bones, nestled against my chest.

Berl had called for help; he had asked me to catch him. While I never did save a drowning child in the Hudson, I averted a disastrous fall that afternoon. The thought was powerful. But I also understood how fortuitous it had been, a matter of inches. Had I lunged a fraction of a second later, things would have unfolded differently. There are times when, instead of coming undone, worlds endure in infinitesimal increments.

Had my father not fallen, I might never have broken his silence about Owen. But I did: I brought up Owen's death an hour later, while the two of us ate lunch on the patio. Leaning over the bowl I had placed in front of him, he dipped his spoon into the soup and slowly brought it to his mouth. This sequence required his full attention. I watched my father as he ate. I scrutinized his face, the skin sagging, the eyes tired, the mouth half-open to the food he could no longer taste. As usual, neither one of us spoke, but that afternoon the silence proved suffocating.

"In a month, it will have been three years," I said. "Three years since Owen died."

I could have spit out these words, a quick, nervous stride across the line my father had drawn. Instead, I spoke them slowly to make sure he heard me.

His head jerked back a little. He looked at me, his spoon suspended at chin level, making sustained eye contact for the first time in months. Then my father let out a groan unlike any I had ever heard, a soft, guttural cry that seemed to originate in a place deep inside him, the place that must have held the shock and consternation, the commiseration, the helplessness I now saw on his face. He could say no more. Though I understood this, I also wished that, just this one time, he had found words.

Berl continued to look at me, and I continued to look at him, although at some point I realized that I was looking past him. He then went back to his soup, and I to mine.

The next day, when we embraced by the front door to mark the end of this visit, I was the one who pulled away first. I had no regrets on the way to the airport, but did worry that Berl and I would never have a meaningful good-bye. I worried about this for weeks—until the day the phone rang and my mother said that my father had fallen again and lost consciousness this time and could I please fly back to Brussels as soon as possible.

TWENTY-ONE

Cory: *How are you doing?*

Monday. His voice a whimper, Berl struggles to answer my questions. I tell him over the phone that I am on my way, but he does not seem to understand. He is fading so fast that I fear he will be incoherent by the time I arrive in Brussels. Still, as I pack, words rise up: follow his cue, tell the truth, touch him, do not feel obliged to say anything profound. Some of these words I gleaned while grieving for Owen in the company of others; others came from the *Tibetan Book of Living and Dying*—someone left us a copy after the accident, and I grab it on the way to the airport. This departure feels like another passage from one state to another, not equal to Owen's death, but still something like a ritual transformation, enacted by words that, like incantations, resonate inside me and fill the plane as it takes off.

Tuesday. Berl's open robe reveals yellow, rubbery skin, shrink-wrapped around the bones. His body has wasted away, but today he is alert and articulate. Propped up in his hospital bed, he asks questions and listens to our answers. The elemental energy that seeped out as he sank inside himself these past months has some-how returned. I feel it the moment I enter his room. I see my father for the first time in months; I hear him.

We all do—my mother and my sister, too. The sound of his voice is familiar, and yet this resurgence makes me question what really happened during these ten months of decline and withdrawal. I try to understand this striking change. Is it the fluids the nurses have been pumping into his veins? A change in his medication? I want to know, but there is no time to consider such matters. Things are moving too fast.

Minutes after my arrival, my father says something so casu-ally and yet purposefully that it takes me several seconds to reg-ister the full meaning of his words. The oncologist will bring test results in the afternoon, he says, and if the news is bad, he will consider suicide.

I do not say anything. None of us do. We stare at my father in silence as he speaks, pauses, and starts up again, laying out his thought process. I feel myself entering his mind while remaining at the edge of something so large I can barely take it in.

Berl reminds us that three years ago, after watching Zosia's decline at the end of her life, he and my mother signed papers allowing doctors to administer a lethal injection should they fall into irreversible coma. A recent Belgian law made this possible. Berl discussed it with us at the time, but almost in passing, as something we ought to know rather than a question on which we had to opine. Now he is talking about suicide, by which he means assisted dying. This, too, is legal under Belgian law: pa-tients afflicted with an untreatable condition and unrelenting pain may request an injection.

My father is speaking in practical terms, as if he were assess-ing a bid for a new patio. He sounds so detached and analytical that I find it difficult to respond emotionally. There is no shock but no sadness either; my father is thinking this through, talking about death, about dying itself and not just assets or funeral plans. I lean forward on the hard chair, elbows resting on my knees, my entire body pulled in his direction.

In the river, there was time to say only one thing and too little time to decide what it would be. Things are different now. I want to ask Berl if he researched the matter. Did you consider the arguments in favor of assisted dying? Did you consult anyone? Also: Are you afraid?

The only question I ask is whether he always knew that his cancer was so serious. He does not answer directly. He says that he has been thinking about this for a while. "You've kept it to yourself," I say. I do not mean it as a reproach; rather, I am surprised and relieved at the thought that his silence has cloaked a richer interior life than I have imagined. If he contemplates death, I think, then perhaps he also makes room for Owen.

The oncologist arrives in the middle of the afternoon. He is a bear of a guy, kind and soft-spoken, with no pretense or unnecessary words. He provides straight information—prognosis, available treatments, possible outcomes—because he is convinced that this is what patients and their families want. I am in awe of this man who fears neither death nor other people's fear of death.

After shaking our hands, he asks to speak with my father alone. In the hallway, I walk toward a bay window that looks over red brick houses. These houses and this neighborhood are familiar; it is in this hospital, a few floors down, that I was born. When my mother returned from the maternity ward, she found a huge, handmade banner in the living room: BERNIE WELCOMES HOME FRANCINE AND STÉPHANE. By the window, I remember my father's softer side and begin to think that he will never return home. Is this what they are talking about in the room? I wonder, again, if he is afraid—as afraid as I would be.

After a few minutes, the oncologist opens the door and calls us in. Standing next to my father, he tells us that his condition will not improve. This leaves three options. The first is a risky, highly toxic regimen he would neither recommend nor choose for himself. The second is to stop treatment and wait it out, with declining quality of life and a life expectancy of two months at most. The final course is what he calls euthanasia.

This is the first time any of us has uttered the word. Coming out of a doctor's mouth, it makes the room feel smaller, the air denser, time palpable. I watch the scene from above: a father in the center, a doctor to his left, the two of them facing the patient's wife and his two grown children. This brings back memories of the accident, when I looked at Owen's body from afar, except that my father is still alive and I am not crouching behind brush.

There are things to know about euthanasia. Patients must request it in writing, more than once, and without external pressure. Also, Belgian law does not grant them the absolute right to euthanasia; doctors may refuse. Before assenting, they must inform patients of their life expectancy, make certain that their suffering is unremitting, lay out all therapeutic options, and confirm their intent to end their life. The doctor must also consult with close relatives.

My father has set in motion a process that is codified and yet heavily reliant on his relationship with his doctor. There is clearly between these two men an intimacy forged out of trust and respect and built upon past understandings. At other times, I might have envied this bond, but not now; I am glad Berl found someone who could help him to make this decision. The oncologist promises to return tomorrow with the latest tumor markers. Let's resume the conversation at that time, he says.

Once the door shuts, Berl tells us he has ruled out further chemo and cannot see the point of palliative care. He does not want to drag things out for weeks or suffer any more. I hear no despondency in his voice. He expected the test results to be bad and knew what he would do upon receiving them. He has made up his mind; this seems clear.

When he asks for our opinions, I realize how little I know about assisted dying beyond the argument about dignity and the counterarguments about vulnerable patients or the sanctity of life. My instincts tell me that my father has the right to control his own end, and so, when my turn comes, I tell him that it is his life and that I will support whatever choice he makes. This is the consensus in the room.

My father says he will ponder the matter overnight and then let us know his decision.

It strikes me that Berl is dying as he lived. So much about his behavior is familiar: the pragmatic approach, the systematic planning, the methodical weighing of variables. And also the focus on his own goals. He needs us close, but he does not ask us point blank whether we would like him to carry on a little longer, or whether his sudden departure troubles us in any way. He does not wonder what his death means for *us* rather than for him. I do not believe that he is under any obligation to ask such questions, but I am not fooling myself either: this death is neither virtuous nor heroic.

But it is unexpected. He says that he is not afraid of dying. He will simply fall asleep and never wake up and finally know what lies on the other side. I cannot understand how he came to accept death, how he achieved something that seemed so far outside his reach. My mother once told me that, whenever she confronted him about his verbal abuse, he replied that he could not change. Now, during his last days, he is venturing beyond himself—in full view.

Later that afternoon, my parents reminisce about trips they have taken over the years, smiling and laughing, returning to places that are theirs alone. I feel as if I am intruding, as if I had walked in on them in bed.

In the early evening, my mother and sister leave to take care of my nephews, and I remain alone with my father, who stares out the window. The day has exhausted him. I offer him some water but he declines so I place the glass on a table within his reach. I fidget, I bring my chair closer to the bed, I rest my feet on the frame. Berl tells me to stop kicking the bed. I had not realized I was kicking his bed.

His eyes shut for long seconds and then reopen. This happens two or three times. He murmurs that he is falling asleep. I ask him whether he would like someone to spend the night with him. He does not answer, so I close the drapes.

As I walk out, I hear his voice asking me to bring his razor tomorrow. He says that he looks as if he has not shaved in a week. In truth, there is only a hint of white stubble on his face.

Wednesday. Berl asks to speak with me as soon as I arrive at the hospital. It is midmorning. I pull up a chair. We are a few feet from each other, closer than Owen and me on the river but not much.

"It's hard to say good-bye, and it will be even harder when the time comes," he says.

In a hushed but assured voice, he says that he is proud of the way I have managed my life, proud of the family I have fashioned, proud of my professional achievements. He thanks me for being a wonderful son. When I reach over to kiss him, his cheeks are moist. "I'm so lucky," he says.

As a child, I found it difficult to believe my mother when she told me my father was proud of me. Why couldn't he say so himself? After the accident, I doubted that I could ever again be seen as a wonderful son. Now I cannot question his sincerity.

Berl does not move. He seems to be waiting for me to speak. I have not prepared anything, but his words make it easy to follow. I thank my father for what he taught me. I tell him that the values he holds dear—honesty, hard work, loyalty—are values I have sought to impart to my children. I also tell him that after I left for college, he gave me freedom and support. It was not an easy transition; I appreciate that.

There must be families in which fathers and sons talk to one another in this way. But Berl never had the need or the ability to do so, not even in the letters he sent me in my twenties. I, in turn, did not trust that such exchanges would prove welcome or safe. I did not even know how to launch such conversations.

Still, my words have not conveyed the full truth about our lives together. I also need to tell him what it means for an eight-year-old to live in a house in which love and violence mesh in seemingly arbitrary ways. I need to tell him he has been a complicated father, which is not the same thing as a bad one. I need to tell him that over time I learned to love him with less fear, but never complete security.

Two days ago, I had reconciled myself to never saying those things. Now I need to find the words. In the past, I would have been too frightened of his rage or my own bitterness to mention his violence. But there is no anger in Berl's hospital room, neither spittle nor narrowed eyes, and so it comes out like this:

"You were a bit tough when I was a kid."

Just this—*a bit tough*—but enough to condense two decades spent in my father's house.

These words hang over the bed, within his reach, like the words that floated before him at dinner in Belarus, when Vera asked if I had other children at home. This time Berl does not tighten his features or look down or let the words pass by. This time he softly says, "Perhaps too tough."

It is not much, but more than I expected, and apparently more than he expected as well because he looks down, as if to give me time to digest his words, or perhaps because he needs time to digest them himself.

I remember how much, as a child and teenager, I had wanted him to say such words, or any others that acknowledged my daily experience. If he had talked to me about his violent mood swings instead of evading my questions, then his life and mine might have followed different courses.

Berl looks up. "You were with me in Belarus," he says. "You saw what kind of world my parents came from."

I move in closer. In Belarus, I saw the old markets and dirt roads, even the river where his mother used to swim, but I realize now that I missed what, maybe, he most wanted me to see: a world of rickety houses in which mothers and fathers and children could love one another despite the deep silences and rough edges. Berl had felt the power of a place and a history that shaped him in ways he did not think he could escape. Despite all of his talk of personal initiative, he seemed to accept this destiny, and now he asked me to understand it.

Maybe this was why he did not travel to Belarus until I pushed him to do so. Maybe he sensed that once he went, he would have to recognize that perhaps he had been too tough.

With my mother and sister in the room, Berl says he spent the night thinking things through. He is ready to go. Now, it is back to practical matters When will the funeral take place? Who must we call?

The oncologist's visit proves anticlimactic. The markers have crept up, but this was expected. My father and his doctor discuss the next step like two partners finalizing a deal that has long been in the works. The doctor explains that some of his colleagues induce a coma that can last days. He prefers a quicker process—five minutes at most. This sometimes shocks the kin, but he sees no point in dragging it out. My father agrees. He turns to my mother and asks about Jewish funerary ritual without really caring. Only one thing matters: that the procedure take place tomorrow.

Once this is settled, my father thanks his doctor for his expertise and human touch. He extends his hand, which the doctor cradles with both of his. Soon their four hands are interlocked above Berl's wan body. This lasts a few seconds and then it is over.

There is a languorous rhythm to the afternoon, an easy drift between banter and nostalgia. Berl grows wistful when recalling how much he admired his older brother as a child. He smiles when my sister and I tease each other as we did when we were little. And he becomes animated when he recalls his early years in Brussels. One of his friends, a Greek bureaucrat, worked at the Common Market in the early 1960s. "He fucked everyone in sight," my father tells me. "He'd say, 'Bernie, the married women are the best. They just don't know about sex in the afternoon. You screw them, get dressed, and return to work reenergized.'" More than the rawness of his words, it is the grin on his face that stays with me. My father still cannot believe that he made it out of Akron.

Dinner comes around five p.m., and so do his stomach cramps. Berl is sapped. Before leaving, I tell him that I love him, and also that I will miss him. "I hope so," he says without irony.

Owen did not say anything during his last moments. In the photograph that Alison took on the river, he looks ahead in silence. He remained quiet when we hit the rocks seconds later. Nor did he speak in the water, when the two of us stared at each other. This may have been Owen's choice; perhaps he was already on his own. More likely, there was time for only one of us to speak, and I told him to keep his feet above water.

When my father and I looked at each other in his hospital room, there was enough time for both of us to speak. Neither one of us had to yell to be heard. Neither one of us told the other to keep his feet above water.

Instead, I heard that I was a good son and Berl heard that he would be missed. This does not happen to everyone. The sun had long set on the Green River when, sitting together in the tent, Alison and I told Owen that we would miss him.

Thursday. Faint orange light enfolds my father's still body. It is early in the morning, and he is lying on his side, wrapped in a blanket. Until he lifts his head, I cannot tell whether he is awake or asleep. He whispers that the pain has been excruciating. "One night too many," he says.

I sit down. At home last night, I jotted down questions for him. Any final advice? Did the euthanasia documents you signed make things easier at the end? And Owen—where do you keep him?

The first question now seems trite and, after all that has been said, pointless. The second feels self-absorbed. As for the last one, I cannot bring myself to force Owen upon him again; I cannot expect that, even now, my father will give me anything more than a groan. But the silence that fills the room this morning is enough. Unlike my father's hollow silence in Belarus, this silence is soft and round. It encompasses the blame he never directed my way, the insinuations he never made about my decisions, the pain he felt and never imposed on me. This silence wraps itself around me and envelops Owen. It shrouds his eternal presence.

It is true that, surrounded by his wife and children, Berl reached a state of equanimity that made me feel Owen's solitude on the river in ways I never have before. It is also true that Berl called me to his side as his son rather than as a bereaved father, that he still has not acknowledged the entirety of my being. But Owen has been with us.

He was there when, winging it, I told Berl what I needed to say and what he could hear about himself as a father. He was also there when Berl showed me that there are good deaths as well as tragic ones. The good deaths take place without fear or violence, without injustice or guilt or shame. The skies do not darken, the thunder does not roar.

Since the accident, I have anticipated my own death as a grisly encounter with Owen, the two of us gasping together just as he may have on the rapids. Now I know that, when my time comes, Berl will be there as well, and this makes all the difference.

Berl and I remain within that silence for a long stretch. When he does talk, it is to ask me when everyone else will arrive. Julian and Alison soon show up, and each speaks with him alone for several minutes. Though Julian does not know about the euthanasia, he understands that his grandfather's life is nearing its end. My mother and my sister then join us, along with Berl's brother and sister-in-law, who flew in from Chicago. It is 10:30; the doctor will arrive at noon.

We set up chairs in a circle around the bed. More banter, more reminiscing—a semblance of normalcy. When Berl trots out the line about eighty good years and one bad one, Julian says that for a baseball team this would be a sweet season. Every few minutes, Berl clicks his tongue on his palate, a tic he inherited from his father. Though he tells stories, he listens more than he speaks. He turns his head to follow the conversation, but a fraction of a second late. He is both with us and already elsewhere.

11:20. Berl takes a sip of water. We talk about the Belgian retail chain for which he worked after leaving the Big Five accounting firm—a chain long sold to a competitor and then liquidated. Its headquarters are being converted into high-end condos. We wonder whether the office with the imposing desk behind which my sister and I sat on Saturday mornings still exists.

11:45. Berl asks for the time. Though no one mentions it, we are all acutely aware of the minutes ticking by. I watch my father, unable to make small talk even though he clearly sees what lies ahead as a liberation.

11:50. I take Julian to the hospital cafeteria and leave him there with lunch money. Alison and I are still trying to protect him. Minutes after I return to the room, the doctor arrives. My father is ready; we all know that he wants quick farewells, a kiss and a swift exit. When my mother leans over the bed, he kisses her then shoos her away, as if to make it easier on the two of them. By chance or design, I am the last one by his side. As I reach toward him, Berl says, "Good-bye, sonny boy." He has not used the nickname since I was a child.

12:05. In the hallway, I watch the doctor roll an IV drip into my father's room and close the door behind him. Alison wishes that one of us were sitting with Berl, but the doctor advised against it and Berl asked to be alone. My mother says that the doctor asked him several times whether he remained committed to his decision.

12:15. The doctor walks out and informs us that my father has gone peacefully. I hug Alison and then my mother, my sister, my aunt and uncle. We all cry, softly, but no one seems devastated. This is, I am certain, because his death was not an act of despair or abandonment. Even in his silence, even when he seemed adrift, he was making choices—especially during his last days, which opened up expanses of feeling that allowed him to trust us, which made space for me to say things I had long wanted to say.

One of the passages I underlined in the *Tibetan Book of Living and Dying* says that for the person who has prepared and practiced, "death comes not as a defeat but as a triumph, the crowning and most glorious moment of life." These are lofty words, and I cannot be certain that my father had prepared or practiced. But I could be wrong.

Friday. Sitting at my father's computer, I compose a group email about his passing that I send my friends. Replies flow in within minutes, extolling a remarkable man, so kind and generous, a man who lived well and died with dignity. How could they not? Though it said nothing about assisted dying, my message retraced his journey from Akron to Brussels to Belarus. There were no family homes to tour in Bobruisk, no tombstones left standing in Parichi, I wrote, but as my father smelled the air and walked on dirt roads that had barely changed over the past century, he appeared to gain a deeper understanding of himself.

He seemed as serene in Belarus as he did during his last days in the hospital. I can now write a story about my father that leaves out violence and anger and still remains truthful.

As I prepare to leave his office, something jumps out at me from his computer screen. It is a folder full of photographs of Owen and Julian. My first impulse is to look away; I still avoid such mementos, I still fear the pain. But Berl sat in this chair and looked at these pictures. I click on the icon.

The first photograph is of Owen at the plate during a Little League game. My stomach tightens. I am not only recovering Owen's presence—and absence—but poking around in Berl's private album, and this feels like a transgression. Still, I go on. There are close-ups and group shots, photographs of Owen as an infant and as a third grader growing into his body. The pain abates. It is not only Owen who is resurfacing in these photographs, but Berl as well, reaching out to his grandson and now to me, as if for the first time.

The window by the desk looks over the garden. Outside, my father's roses sway by the steps on which he lost his balance just a few weeks ago. This is what I see when, distracted by a summer breeze, I take my eyes off the screen. But I do not do so for long because inside the house there are no falls—just Owen, Berl, and me, standing together beyond the confines of death and life.

PART

III

End Stories

TWENTY-TWO

Thomas: *My story is in my head*

Owen went so fast and violently, Berl so slowly and deliberately—in slow motion almost—that, in both cases, it was impossible to register what was happening until it was over. Back in New York, I revisited those four days with my father. I had seen him contemplate death; I had listened as he discussed matters we had avoided until then. As I relived all of this, I kept picturing the two of us with Owen—together during his last moments.

And yet, what had really happened in Brussels? I wondered because I knew how much I longed for a transformative story about the accident and our life without Owen and now without Berl. That story would bring some coherence to the chaos of our lives and maybe offset Owen's absence in some minute way. Only weeks after the accident, I had written in my journal: "Nothingness will not stand."

As a historian, I resisted nothingness by becoming a chronicler of our own lives, documenting the aftermath of this catastrophe with precision. I had to create a comprehensive record of what happens on a river, inside a family, and within the broader world when a child dies at the start of the third millennium.

Yet I also sought to shape our experiences into a meaningful narrative, and part of me worried that such impulses would distort our family's experience—not just Owen's and mine, but Alison's and Julian's and my father's as well. If our lives became nothing but a story, or rather nothing but my story, governed by what I had observed and overlooked, what I had registered and forgotten, would this chronicle deserve any credence? Could I trust my own words?

Perhaps I had only seen what I needed to see in Brussels: Berl and I accepting the idea of change and changing and precipitating change together, with our sons by our sides. This was after all what I had awaited: a story of posttraumatic growth and redemption in which sons and fathers came together without anger or shame. I told myself that I had not invented or exaggerated or omitted anything essential, but I also knew that things might have gone missing.

Still, I could not dismiss the story that had begun in Belarus and ended in Belgium. Without it, there was nothing but a world in which children vanish, parents live with random abductions, and all deaths prove equally tragic. After his daughter succumbed to pneumonia, Paul Gauguin wrote that "on the news of my poor Aline's death I doubted everything, I gave a defiant laugh. What use are virtue, work, courage, intelligence?" I, too, had doubted all this, along with expert knowledge and our ability to safeguard what we hold dearest. I even doubted facets of the stories I had been composing since Owen died. But I could not deny their force or their necessity.

After my return from Brussels, I did things that had become impossible after the accident. I followed the route that Owen, Julian, and I used to take to school in the morning and allowed myself to feel the city's energy uncoil. I walked by a father holding his eight-year-old son by the hand and, instead of flinching, let the scene seep through my body. While every mishap continued to carry the possibility of devastation, I also talked to Julian about his new high school and peered into his future. Whether all this became possible because of what had happened in Belarus and Brussels, or because of how I had chosen to frame these events, I felt something akin to a release.

More than three years had now elapsed since the accident, and Alison continued to mourn fearlessly. One day, I watched her approach two of Owen's classmates with the certainty that, however much her presence might unsettle them, they would happily recall sleepovers and morning waffles with their dead friend. Alison needed to make sure that a decade hence these boys would still find a place for Owen within their lives. In other situations, though, she protected herself in ways I had never noticed before. She sometimes walked toward Owen's room and turned around at the last minute, or took a detour to avoid passing by his school at pickup time.

I could not anticipate how Alison would react, therefore, when I asked her to listen as I read something I had written about the accident. I had been working on this book for a few months, writing in Owen's room, which I had avoided for so long, and occasionally I read her a paragraph or two to test the voice, the tone, the way she came across. These paragraphs revolved around grief rather than the accident, however. Now I wanted to read her a passage about the river.

Alison lay down on Owen's bed while I pulled up a chair and placed my computer on my lap. For a few minutes, my voice filled the room, uninterrupted. Then Alison sat up and asked me to stop. She could not listen anymore—not right then, she said. My words did not merely summon images of the river;

they transported her back to Disaster Falls, causing her to relive everything that had happened that day. She found this unbearable.

Alison eventually read the entire manuscript. She did so at a time, a place, and a pace of her choosing. The chapters on the river were the most difficult, but she read them too. In fact, Alison read the manuscript three times, allowing herself to do what she still refrained from doing on her own: to return to the rapids.

Around the same time, Alison offered to share other things the medium had told her about Owen. My instinct was to say no. I still did not want to lose myself in that magical universe. And yet, on a bike ride through Columbia County, New York, I told Alison to go ahead. Perhaps I wanted to see what would happen if I opened myself to her version of the accident. Or perhaps I wanted to thank Alison for allowing me to write a story that was not mine alone.

"I won't tell you everything," Alison said, "but the medium saw rocks. She said Owen hit his head and fell unconscious."

Alison related this as we approached a hill. We both stood on our bikes and pedaled harder—too hard to talk but not to carry the medium's image of Owen. At the top, Alison said that she found it comforting to hear that Owen had been unconscious. It meant that he had suffered less.

"Owen was happy that day," Alison said. "There was no pain."

We rode in silence among peach orchards and faded red barns, within earshot of streams that we still elected not to hear. Had I encouraged Alison to say more, she would have told me Owen did not want us to blame ourselves. He had said this to the medium, and also that Alison could not have protected him, and that the accident had not been my fault. Owen told the medium he loved me.

Alison relayed all this some time later. That afternoon I did not ask her for more detail but neither did I object (at least, not for long or with conviction) that the medium could have learned about us online and made up the rest. Nor did I tell Alison that all bereaved parents want to hear about love rather than pain when it comes to their children—no wonder the medium had framed it that way. This thought did not cross my mind.

Instead, I found comfort in the story, forceful and necessary, that Alison had been holding for a long time on her own. Whether events on the river had taken place that way or not hardly mattered at that moment. Alison and I could choose to make this story our own; we could compose it together.

TWENTY-THREE

Nicky: *How did he hurt himself?*

The story of the accident could have ended where I left it. But, after reading an early version, a friend asked about our lawsuit. Why had I not mentioned it?

Alison and I had filed a civil suit soon after the Moffat County Sheriff's Office deemed Owen's death an accident. The legal process lasted close to two years and yet I had said nothing about litigation. Even after my friend asked, I left it out of the manuscript I sent to my publisher. My editor knew nothing, and so she asked why Alison and I had chosen not to sue.

I could not tell her that my omission had been inadvertent because it had not been. But neither was it a considered decision. I had simply allowed myself to believe that legal constraints forbade me from discussing the suit, its resolution, or even the grounds of our complaint. It would have been a simple matter to verify—a quick call to our lawyer—but what if he told me I could not discuss some facets of the accident? I would have to leave out elements of my story.

And what if, on the contrary, he replied that I could disclose everything? Then there would be no external justification for my omission. I would have to return to the rapids according to a timetable and from vantage points that were not mine; I would have to revisit the accident through an adversarial legal process; and I would have to confront the failings of others in ways I had not done until now. This would be another story altogether.

I did not make that phone call until my friend and my editor asked. Then I found out that, with the exception of the final terms, I could indeed disclose it all.

How do I write, then, about a legal process that seemed vain and yet necessary?

Alison and I sued because Owen's death had been unfair, to obtain some form of justice—we owed it to Owen—and to make it safer to run the Green. This led us to target the rafting company rather than Delma or Kris. We had expected more from the two of them on the lookout, in the rapids, throughout the search effort, and during the twenty-fours we then spent in the canyon. We wished they had not disappeared the moment Owen vanished from view. We would have liked to hear them say they were sorry about his death. But taking them to court seemed pointless. Responsibility ultimately lay with the corporation that devised procedures and trained its staff.

Still, our expectations for reparation were low. We knew the odds were against structural change in a region and an industry that have long resisted regulation. When I called Dinosaur National Monument after the accident to find out what kinds of canoes and duckies were allowed on rapids, the river manager told me that outfitters make such decisions on their own. "We can't tell people what to do or not do," she said.

After deaths such as this one, parents sometimes set up nonprofits, launch petitions, lobby officials, and raise money to enact change. Personal catastrophe can breed activism. But the accident depleted my inner resources and made me turn inward rather than outward. I did not have it in me to fight an industry and a culture that prizes the free, unregulated life—human beings and nature in unfettered communion.

Alison and I remained passive throughout the process. The two of us barely discussed it, and shared little with Julian, who, we later learned, felt excluded. The few relatives and friends whom we told heard tidbits such as "we are talking to our lawyer today." No one asked about a matter that raised uncomfortable questions about fault and responsibility. Even my journal contains few entries about the matter, as if I had excised it from my life.

We hired an attorney from Los Angeles. Beyond the practical rationale—the rafting company was incorporated in California—this physical distance enabled us to remain detached from the process. His name was Moses, and I imagined him tapping divine powers to part waters and lead us to the other side. During occasional phone calls, the grave, warm, disembodied voice of Moses remained as remote as I needed it to be.

Early on, Moses asked us to write down everything that we remembered of the accident. Both of us stalled. Alison left her narrative on her hard drive for weeks. When she finally emailed it to Moses, she wrote that the more she thought about the accident, the less she understood what case the opposing attorneys could build. "Do you feel the same way, or am I deluded?" she asked.

How do I write about a process that will flatten Owen?

The case revolved around the death of a child on a trip that had been advertised as a family vacation. At issue was the risk we assumed by signing the company's release, and the risk the outfitters had to make public and curtail. Experts would have to determine whether a novice boater and an eight-year-old should have risked riding Class III rapids in a ducky.

Litigation would force us to reexamine Disaster Falls in clinical detail. A trial would force upon us the autopsy we had declined: a legal, expertise-driven autopsy, carried out through maps and photographs and testimony. Owen was bound to vanish: a boy reduced to a corpse, an exhibit, a victim whose financial value actuaries would appraise. How could he remain visible once future earnings, accumulations, and loss of services became the order of the day?

Do I write that I was terrified?

The opposing lawyers would come after me—for signing the release, for allowing Owen to board the ducky after scouting the falls, and, I imagined, for letting the current take us to the right instead of the left of No-Name Island. I expected a barrage of hostile questions from attorneys, a company, that entire industry and culture.

Once the discussion moved to fault and neglect and carelessness, the pursuit of justice would morph into self-defense and a quest for retribution. There would be no way to resist anger— the kind of anger that leaves nothing standing in its wake, certainly not a story in which beauty somehow enclosed horror.

Once thoughts of negligent and unnecessary death filled my days, how would I remain open to the world? How would I look toward the future with Alison and bequeath anything of substance to Julian?

People around me had expressed anger over the years. Julian had voiced his wrath at the river outfitters and the entire state of Utah. One of Owen's Little League coaches had told me she felt it whenever she drove by the Esopus Creek in the Catskills. She was now angry at all rivers, she said. I could understand such feelings, but also remembered the bereaved couple that had visited us during the early weeks. They had sued as well, and their rage seemed to leave room for little else in their lives. I continued to believe that anger had to be tamed, stifled, harnessed, pushed out, or rather pushed under. While writing my narrative of the accident, I began formulating questions for the outfitters. Why do they allow children in duckies on rapids? Why had we not been informed of the comparative risks in duckies and rafts? Why had the guides not taught us how to maneuver duckies in rapids? Why had the scouting begun before everyone was assembled? Why were there so many duckies on the river—and no guides in kayaks behind us? Why did no raft move in to look for Owen? Why did no one throw a rope? And why did the recovery focus on land, without considering the worst-case scenario, namely that Owen was still in the water?

Compiling these questions, arranging them into some kind of logical progression, provided a temporary reprieve, a measure of control over the world. But as I composed this indictment (for this is what it was), I could feel myself becoming an enraged father, falling to the fury he cannot contain.

I completed the narrative as fast as I could and sent it off to Moses.

There is no reason to manufacture suspense. The insurers dragged out the process until Moses deposed the rafting company's director. He emailed us a one-paragraph summary that evening, explaining why he thought the deposition would work in our favor. Indeed, the insurers promptly submitted a new offer for a settlement, which we considered and then accepted. We did so to protect Julian, protect ourselves, and, in my case, shield my-self from anger. "I needed the suit to happen," Alison said, "but I want it to go away."

Neither one of us read the deposition, even though Moses emailed us a transcript. Occasionally I highlighted the file name with my cursor, imagining what I might feel and learn if I clicked. The questions and the answers would circle Utah and Colorado and then slice into Dinosaur, into Lodore and the Green and then Disaster Falls, in and out and back in again— further in until there was nowhere left to go.

But I could not write about the suit without reading the de-position, which is why, a day after making that call to Moses and five years after the settlement, I returned to the Woodstock stu-dio in which I had written Owen's eulogy. I positioned my laptop by the large window overlooking the forest and the bluestone quarry that has been dormant for a century. At that moment, its mounds of mossy stone, slabs piled up in uncertain stacks, did not speak of labor or a changing local economy. All I saw as I opened the file was a place frozen in time, nature silencing human history.

Superior Court of the State of California for the County of Calav-eras. Stéphane Gerson, Alison Gerson, and the estate of Owen Ger-son, plaintiffs. Deposition commencing at 1:24 p.m. and ending at 5:40 p.m.

One hundred and sixty-two pages, including sworn affirma-tion under penalty of perjury, verification by the certified short-hand reporter, and errata sheet.

The first exchanges are polite, even amiable. Moses asks ques-tions, sometimes the opposing lawyer interrupts a line of ques-tioning, but mostly the company director concedes one point after another. He does not present them as concessions, though. They are just facts, devoid of moral content.

I begin taking notes:

- No formal protocol to assess level of guides or train them.
- Cannot say when safety instructions were given to guides or what was said during said meetings.
- Knew about the fatality a few years before the accident, the tourist who drowned after foot entrapment. Same river, but different outfitter and different Class III rapids. Never inquired about exact circumstances.
- Trip leader's swift-water rescue certification expired months before the accident. Certification applies to "hazardous conditions involving whitewater" (director).

I condense what he has to say into bullet points—another list, another compilation of facts, but this one with moral content. The answers Moses elicits during the first hour of the deposition make it impossible to speak any longer of haphazard oversights or shortcomings. An underlying logic ties these facts together. Moving back and forth in the transcript, putting different passages in dialogue with one another, I piece together this logic as if it were one of the ideologies I have come across as a historian, something that can be understood even without comprehending its ethical foundation.

What I uncover is so foreign that I can no longer digest it in bullet points. I have to copy entire passages.

Q *What do you believe to be the primary purpose of the guide in terms of the passengers, the guide's role and the passenger's role, in going through these rapids?*

A *To provide a quality experience taking passengers downriver,*

*supplying equipment, giving instruction, preparing meals, al-
lowing people to come from all over the country, and actually
from all over the world, to go down the various rivers.*

Q *And to do it safely?*

A *Hopefully to do it safely.*

Q *Wouldn't you agree with me that the primary function of the
guide is not to ensure that the person is having fun but to make
sure that the person gets from point A to point B safely?*

A *It's a tough question. In general, I would say a guide should help
the passengers have a safe trip down the river. We do not try to
hold out to passengers that this is a safe trip. We do not charac-
terize it as one that they can choose without concern for safety.
I think it is very obvious to everybody looking at this rapid that
this rapid has a reasonably high percentage risk of capsizing.*

I discern something startling: the assumption that the ability
to assess risk is innate, evenly distributed among all human beings. Regardless of our training or profession, regardless of our
previous experiences or degree of familiarity with, say, the West
and its rapids, we share the same ability to gauge risk and make
decisions accordingly.

Pressed by Moses, the director acknowledges the higher risks
for duckies on Class III rapids. He provides numbers: a ducky
has a 25 to 35 percent chance of capsizing on Disaster Falls, a
raft less than 5 percent. He knows this, and his guides may have
known it as well. But no one in the company shared these statistics with the men and women and children they led down the
river.

Q *Do you know if there are any safety discussions the night before
that address or give information to the passengers about whether
they could use an inflatable kayak in Disaster Falls; that is, how*

hard it is, how easy it is, whether it could capsize, what happens if it capsizes, what you do, whether—whether it's suitable for a novice or not suitable? Any conversation about those issues the night before?

A *To the best of my knowledge, that is not part of that discussion. And the reason is because the person has to see this rapid to think if they want to go through this rapid or not.*

No such discussion took place during the scouting either. The director concedes this as well. People would figure it out on their own. It is a matter of common sense—*very obvious to everybody.*

Q *Does the company, your company, do any kind of determination to ensure that the individuals are knowledgeable with respect to how to properly navigate Disaster Falls?*

A *I would say the answer has to be no.*

I need to digest this, so I stand up, I step outside, I walk over to the quarry. Under the yellow leaves, the faded blues and greens of the stone blend into the hues of the river. There is, after all, sense to be made of what happened that day. Specific notions of risk, common sense, and personal responsibility explain why Delma and Kris acted as they did. Because this conception of risk was not ours, because we could not even imagine it before leaving for Utah, Alison and I had failed to understand the company's promotional brochures. When we read that the trip was "open to children seven and up" and staffed by "skilled, knowledgeable, professional guides," we concluded that they had vetted the rapids for every age, every skill level, every type of vessel. We trusted that outfitters had assessed risk on our behalf.

But this was a complete misreading. The company was only

promising to bring us to the rapids. Once there, we would look at the water and, on the basis of what we saw, make an instinctive determination of risk.

I now understand what I have desperately sought to comprehend since that day. The sudden rise in danger after lunch, our misgivings on the lookout, the guides' reluctance to validate our doubts when we asked them if the rapids were safe—all of this fits within the company's logic. Alison and I felt as though we had been left to our own devices because we had been. The director did not say otherwise in his deposition; he never claimed that his staff provided information or made recommendations that we ignored. We had not been deluded.

This realization provides no closure, but it does confirm what I sensed and yet refused to believe when guilt became the thread of my personal horror story. I detect a slight shift inside me; my body feels lighter and also stronger.

The deposition is not over. In the studio, I place my laptop on a high shelf and read while standing, hands in my pockets to make myself the narrowest of targets. After three hours, Moses changes tack. He draws the director into a discussion of corporate practices that, like so much in this testimony, could not fit in the summary he emailed us at the time.

Q *You have marketing that's targeted for families with young children?*

A *I don't know what the question means. I don't consider it marketing. We are putting information out there, and people determine that they want to do one of our trips.*

Q *Well, you have a marketing director?*

A *We have a marketing director.*

Q *What do you understand the word "marketing" to mean?*

A *Disseminating information so people can make a good determination about whether this is an activity that they want to engage in . . .*

Q *You're a profit—you're not a non-profit organization, are you?*

A *We are formed as a profit-making entity.*

Q *And you increased your number of trips from twenty to forty [in 2007, a year before the accident] because you could make a greater profit on forty trips than you could on twenty trips?*

A *That is an assertion by you. And in general conversation, I would say that is one of the things that motivate us at the company. But there's another strong component, because we believe we are imparting something to people. We are sharing something valuable with people.*

Q *You charge people to go on the trip?*

A *Yes.*

Q *You charge for an adult, correct?*

A *Yes.*

Q *You charge for a child?*

A *Yes.*

Q *And the more people who come on your trips, the more money you make?*

Defense attorney: *Well, objection. That assumes facts not in evidence. It doesn't consider overhead and insurance and all the other aspects of doing business.*

Q *You're a profit-making venture; we've established that.*

A *We are a venture that seeks to make a profit.*

Q *And the more people who pay you and go on your trips, the more money potentially you are going to make, right?*

A *Potentially, yes. But there are lots of variables in terms of the operation of a trip.*

Q *You would agree with me, sir, putting aside the variables of the*
   operation of a trip, that the more people who use your product,
   which is rafting trips, the more money that [your company] can
   make, is that true?
Defense attorney: *First of all, I have given you some latitude to go*
   beyond the deposition notices and—
Q *This is just simple stuff.*
Defense attorney: *Well, it's not simple stuff. It's—well, one, it's been*
   asked and answered; two, you are getting really far afield of the
   notices; and, three, it's irrelevant to any issue in this case.
Q *It goes to the very heart of everything we're talking about . . .*
Defense attorney: *Counsel, I'm—*
Q *He can say "yes" or "no."*
Defense attorney: *I'm not going to let him answer the question.*

As I take this in, abstract notions like *political economy of risk*
come to mind. I remember reading about the 1906 San Francisco earthquake, depicted by politicians and economic leaders
as a chance occurrence against which little could have been done.
These men deemed risk unavoidable, but remained silent about
the dangers of new construction, which had rendered some
San Franciscans more vulnerable than others. Without saying
so, they set allowable levels of risk. While the world has always
been a dangerous place, the late capitalist era seems to expose
populations to risks—cities built on fault lines, flood-zone devel-
opments, crop-dusted vegetables—that remain unseen or unac-
knowledged. When something goes wrong, nature is the culprit.
The human factor remains invisible.

A personal injury lawyer tripped up a rafting executive in his
own contradictions; he made him concede that his company kept
silent about the risks to which it exposed its clients. The director
and his company were either denying the consequences of their

actions or—more likely—so caught up in their own logic, their
own political economy of risk, that they could not see those consequences, not even when they came into glaring view, not even
when a child slipped away and died.

It is not about an earthquake zone that they are keeping silent. It is about Owen.

I step away again.

Outside the window, the quarry has taken on a darker shade.
I see something different now in its debris: a remnant from another era in which workers were subjected to forms of risk they
did not comprehend because these risks were not made compre-
hensible.

When I behaved as the director's logic stipulated that I
should—look at the rapids, feel fear—I did not obtain the information I needed to make the right decision. Afterward, I shoul-
dered the responsibility alone, as if this were the lot of the father
whose son had been lost on the river, the father who had to expi-
ate his guilt. I referred to Owen's death as an accident; I still do.
In truth, Owen was not seen at the end of his life. No one had
been looking, except for Alison and Julian in their rafts, except
for me, gazing into Owen's eyes until it came time to let go. It
was not the river that killed Owen after all.

Anger runs through me. I cannot deny its presence.

When Moses emailed us his summary of the deposition, I
had felt a sudden desire to crush the company, an impulse whose
violence left me reeling. There were good reasons to cast it aside
and eschew this rage. Taking the company to court to fulfill
what Alison called a fantasy of financial ruination would in the
end make us feel worse. There were good reasons to stay away
from the suit, good reasons not to write about it.

But the anger I feel within me now is different from the
anger I witnessed when that bereaved couple visited our house

and different from the anger I experienced at home while growing up. It is targeted rather than all-encompassing, measured
rather than impulsive. It matches the outrage of Owen's death
without reenacting its violence. Perhaps this is what justice looks
like. I cannot be certain; there are compelling arguments for justice that exclude anger. Vengeance cannot after all restore what
was lost; lashing out, whether in pain or fury or hate, comes at a
cost for the party that seeks payback.

Still, after circling Disaster Falls for years, it suddenly hits me
that shunning all forms of anger bears costs of its own. Without
anger, can I recognize the full injustice of Owen's death?

Moses is almost done, but not quite. During the last half hour,
he revisits the scouting in painstaking detail. He has kept this for
the end, as if to prepare us.

Q *What is your understanding of how your company describes the
Class III rapids on the—to prospective consumers on Disaster
Falls?*

A *My understanding is that we don't make much effort to go into
educating the client about Disaster Falls other than to give them
the name of the rapid.*

Q *Okay. And would it be correct that the only time any effort is
made to educate the client, using your phrasing, is at the time when
you're—you've got the client and you're scouting the rapid?*

A *I think that's fair to say, yes.*

Q *And what actually is said to the client at that point is—you're
not aware of that?*

A *I'm not aware of that. But I've talked to many kids, having been
a guide, and a kid will look at this rapid, and they will be scared
of it.*

I read this last sentence several times, slower and slower until the words split apart and between them—between *guide* and *kid* and *rapid* and *scared*—there is just enough space to glimpse Owen on the lookout, Owen staring at rapids that might have been scary from his vantage point, but not scarier than a roller coaster, not scary enough to make him suspect he would capsize and end up alone in these rapids, not scary enough to overrule the guides and the parents who told him that all would be okay, not scary enough to deter a boy who never knew whether on any given day he would submit to his fears or overcome them.

Q *Have you given that information, that a child would be scared of this, to your area managers so that they could work with the guides and educate the children about what they're going to be going through and how to do it safely?*

A *No. I believe it is self-evident to any child—almost any child, any adult, when they look at this rapid that they would know this rapid has something to be fearful about.*

Q *And given that you believe that it had something to be fearful about, do you believe that this rapid poses a risk of death?*

A *I would say, yes, this rapid poses a risk of death . . .*

Q *Do you instruct your guides to tell the passengers on—when they're scouting this area, that this—these rapids pose a risk of death?*

A *No. But it is very clear—*

I want to tell the director that nothing is very clear in such situations, least of all the inner life of an eight-year-old. But would he understand? I let his words seep out into the surrounding woods.

This leaves Owen by the gushing waters.

Owen left to decide if the whole thing looks runnable.

Owen left to assess risk of death.

Owen left to determine whether the emotions he feels at this moment—fear or excitement or perhaps something else altogether—should govern what he says to the father who, as he put it in his third-grade journal, is scared a lot. Owen is so alone that I want to do now what I did not do on the river. I want to rush over, hold his body, kiss his cheeks, and also scream, wail, and then fall to the ground, flattened on the dirt.

I do not scream, I do not wail. But I drop to my knees in the studio, body folded, face on the floor, hands behind my neck. I remain that way for a long time. Then I stand up, straighten my back, and for the first time I hold everything at once: the political economy of rafting trips, the necessary anger, and the indelible sadness of it all.

This is not much when it comes to a disaster of cosmic magnitude, a disaster without justice for Owen, a disaster whose story is bound to remain insufficient. But as I look out one last time at the quarry, now shapeless and purple in the crepuscular forest, something inside me feels complete.

TWENTY-FOUR

Ryan: *How do you feel now?*

J ulian was in college by the time I read the deposition. When we began touring campuses, around his sixteenth birthday, he was leading the full life of a teenager, flourishing in his new high school. One evening, he folded pillows under his covers, told Alison that Owen was with him, and asked her to kiss them both good night. It may have been when things went well, when he was forging ahead, that Julian had to touch base with his brother.

Over time Julian spoke about Owen less, especially at school, where he only told a handful of friends that he had a brother. Julian needed to reinvent himself as someone else besides the kid who had lost his only sibling. I knew this, and so did Alison, but we still winced when, returning home after a night out, we found our framed photographs of Owen piled on our bedroom dresser. Before inviting friends over, Julian had cleared the living room of all signs of his brother's existence. It was too much for the other kids, Julian said, too awkward with girls.

Alison and I wondered how Julian would eventually look back upon the years that had immediately followed the accident. This would become a short chapter in his life, all things considered. In a senior-year English essay, he explained that he had felt so alone during the first year. "My parents, wracked with grief, did their best to console me, but I often found myself doing the consoling," he wrote. Perhaps he still felt the same with college looming and worried about leaving us on our own, without anyone checking in every day. Or perhaps he wondered what he would do now that he no longer had to console his parents. It is also possible that Alison and I were the only ones fretting about such matters, late in the evening, while returning photographs of Owen to our walls and bookshelves.

We encouraged Julian to choose an out-of-state college in order to decide for himself who should learn about Owen. We did not tell him, however, how much his impending departure frightened us. Alison's mediations and my scholarship still felt too hollow or perfunctory to provide direction or purpose. There were still days when it seemed as if one enterprise alone, ensuring Julian's well-being, lay within our reach.

Regardless, Julian would leave home, and the two of us would stay. We would stay with Owen, keeping his room dust-free while following the growth of the Japanese maple we had planted in his memory. We would stay in case one of his grade-school friends dropped by without warning, and also in case Owen came out of his room one night and stood in the living room doorway, alone and silent until one of us noticed and smiled and got up to take his hand and walk him back to bed, where darkness and sleep awaited, as foreboding that night as every other night.

Owen did make an appearance one night. In a dream, I spotted him outside a movie theater. I did not recognize him at first, but there he was, walking with friends. When I ran over to embrace him, he seemed pleased to see me but distant, as if he could not remember what it had been like to live with us. When I recounted this dream to Alison the next morning, I left out one thing because it seemed almost indecent. As I ran toward Owen, I had felt not only joy and incredulity, but also euphoria: Owen's story would end with his return from the dead. It would be a story for the ages, a miracle, atonement for the deaths of all children, the antidote to all horror stories.

My dream did not come true. But a month later Alison missed her period. She did not really believe she was pregnant, not at age forty-six. Women of her age have less than a 1 percent chance of natural pregnancy. The likelihood is even lower for those who, like Alison, have a history of fibroids, which can enlarge the uterus and make it difficult for embryos to implant. I had learned these statistics when we tried to conceive a few months after the accident. The two of us felt that something fundamental had been interrupted. We were not done parenting, and we worried about Julian's solitude.

Choosing to have another child had not been straightforward. Wherever I looked, I saw toddlers running unsupervised before garage entrances and children roller-blading down streets that flowed into busy thoroughfares. Some evolutionary mechanism must prevent parents from understanding exactly what it means to release a child into the world. Once this mechanism breaks down, it seems inconceivable that anyone would take on such a responsibility. Would we hold a celebration—a celebration for ourselves—once our new child reached the age of nine?

Also: Were we simply trying to replace Owen? And did we deserve another child?

If Alison asked such questions the first year, she kept them to herself. She also refused to let my apprehension about the health risks of midlife pregnancy stop us. "You can't live in fear," she said before undergoing the first of three procedures to remove her fibroids. Soon afterward, Julian (age twelve at the time) over-heard us discussing the matter and asked whether we were re-ally planning to have another child. The news threw him into a frenzy. He fired off one counterargument after another, as if he had uncovered a plot he might still disrupt through swift action. His friends would tease him, he said. The baby would keep him up at night. His schoolwork would suffer. Pregnant women of Alison's age look ridiculous. We could not replace Owen. And finally: "Things are so good now between the three of us." Julian could not envision another disruption of our family unit.

Alison and I tried conceiving for a year, until things petered out without either one of us saying much about it. We did not go back to contraception at the end of that year, but neither did we opt for invasive procedures, hormones, injections, in vitro fertilization, egg donors, surrogate mothers, or adoption. It was not that we decided against any of it. It just happened that way because neither one of us had enough strength or confidence to convince the other that another child would resolve anything. We chose by not choosing.

Three years later, Alison purchased a pregnancy test one morning and asked her gynecologist for confirmation that same afternoon.

The prospect of a baby reopened a spigot of emotions about the contours of our family. I could not yet detect the lighter breath, the larger footprint, the emboldened sense of self I associated with a new child. But I did not feel quite as old anymore. I could now imagine a world that did not revolve around death.

When we told Julian about the pregnancy, he asked—seriously and playfully—how this could have happened given that he was always around the house. The news pleased him, not least because, as he put it, the baby would give Alison and me something to do after he left. Julian could not recall his earlier misgivings about a new child, not even when we reminded him.

When we told friends and relatives that we were expecting another child, they used words like *magical, mythic,* and *miraculous.* One deemed it biblical, as if Alison had joined the elderly Sarah, mother of Isaac, and Elizabeth, mother of St. John the Baptist. Another friend said he might start believing in some force at work in the universe. "You are having another kid, you will never die."

More than one friend told me I now had the ending to my story. The end imbues the story with its moral; it is "everywhere the chief thing," Aristotle famously wrote. Short of Owen returning, this was indeed the most satisfying conclusion to a tale about a dead boy and his family. Over the years, I had heard about bereaved parents who regained joy after having another baby. I heard it secondhand, never from the parents themselves, but is it not true that a new child alone can compensate? People now told us they felt pure happiness for us, a kind of peace they had not known since Owen died. An acquaintance confided that she had been so sorry for us when she heard about the accident. "But now! . . ."

No one forgot about Owen, but our family story seemed to morph all too easily into a wondrous fantasy, filled with the illusion of reparation and the expectation of renewal. "Your life has become a novel that writes itself," a friend said. This ending was also a beginning, but how were we to launch something new without believing in the possibility of fresh starts, freed from the past? How would we carry the memory of a dead child while remaining open to the possibilities of a new life?

I wondered whether I would allow myself to experience the

full immersion in parenthood that I observed in young couples. If so, where would this leave Owen? If not, if loyalty to his memory and fear of pain held me back, what kind of father would I be this time around? Children deserve insouciance and the belief in a better future and a world in which mistakes do not necessarily yield disasters.

These qualms were not mine alone. Alison was not certain she would dare to love another child with abandon. She was moved after hearing the baby's heartbeat for the first time but also found the prospect of a new life daunting. Julian grew edgy and explained that it was because Alison and I were starting a new family just as he left home. For the first time since the accident, we had begun something without him. Secrecy reigned in the house, Julian said.

And yet, the pull proved so strong. Alison and I allowed ourselves to picture Julian sharing family stories with his new sibling. Julian in turn joined us in conversations about the baby. The day he submitted his first college application, he put his hand on Alison's belly to feel the fetus kick. By then, Alison was entertaining the idea that Owen had waited until we were ready to send us this child.

Alison looked different, too. Her cheeks had filled in, her eyes had softened, her dark hair caressed the back of her neck and framed a face that had regained its proportions. After meeting Alison for the first time, an older woman told her she had a remarkably open face. It was so open, this woman said, that strangers must feel compelled to tell her everything.

All I could tell Alison when she spoke of feeling daunted was that I would not be able to protect this child—another boy, as it turned out—from the perils of the world or assure him that a long life lay ahead. I might never look at his face without searching for traces of Owen's features. Until he reached the age of eight, I might remain unable to touch his body without picturing Owen's in the background. And one day I would lose him—not a physical loss with any luck, but a loss nonetheless, perhaps sudden or more likely at the end of a slow process, an accretion of tiny daily losses that escape detection. I could hold this child's hand as tightly as I wanted in subway stations and atop canyons, and it still would not change a thing.

But before that moment, there was another opportunity to become a father—not necessarily better than Berl, but perhaps as open as he had been during his last days. In the story that filled my head as the birth approached, I allowed this boy to fall and fail, casting off the illusion that I could always protect him. In this story, I raised him without having to chronicle our lives or shape his into a narrative. In this story, Owen and I walked together at all hours, and his presence gave me enough courage to teach his younger brother to become a happy man.

EPILOGUE

Samantha: *What did you do*
on Owen's birthday?

On his ninth birthday, three months after the accident, we shared photographs and memories. Afterward, we wrote notes on a balloon that we released from a balcony and watched vanish over the skyline. It was difficult to let go. Zosia died that day.

On Owen's tenth birthday, night was already falling when we visited the cemetery, so we turned on the car's headlights. We stood around the grave, our shadows painted on the flat gray stone.

On his eleventh birthday, Julian told us that everything had changed. So many things are now worse, he said.

On his twelfth birthday, we looked at pictures but barely spoke of Owen. It seemed difficult to take hold of him without rituals.

I cannot recall what we did on Owen's thirteenth birthday. That would have been his bar mitzvah.

Owen's fourteenth birthday fell one month before Alison's due date and a week before the day we had set to repaint his bedroom, which would become the baby's. We still had to empty his drawers, pack up his books, remove his posters, and place the postcards and photographs that Owen had pinned above his desk into an envelope for safekeeping. Alison had wanted to do this for weeks, but I had resisted. I was not done with this book, which I continued to write in Owen's room. Another story was about to begin, connected but separate. I needed to finish this one first.

When Alison asked if I had anything in mind for this birthday, I thought of the trip that Owen and I had taken to the Baseball Hall of Fame a month before the accident. Cooperstown loomed as a place of childlike innocence, intimacy, and discovery. That was where the two of us had talked about both planning and winging it—where I had learned about Owen's relationship to the world and reconsidered my own. After the accident, I had kept away from Cooperstown. I found it difficult to pick up the wooden bat, black and red with golden engraving, that Owen had chosen in a souvenir shop during that visit. But once we found out about Alison's pregnancy, I vowed to return before the birth. This left little time.

In the end, I did not go to Cooperstown. The trip remained too fraught, too full of imponderables. Five years was not enough time. I did not berate myself, but I wished that I had made it back. The trip would have provided a fitting coda, especially if I could sit in the bleachers in which Owen and I had sat and open photo albums for the first time.

But regret did not linger because Owen was now inscribed within a story and a history in which a single day stretched across centuries and all generations responded to a man-made disaster by coming together around an eight-year-old boy. This story had to be written in order to be read, again and again, until nothing separated the past from the present, until nothing separated a world without Owen from a world that kept the uncertainty of his presence ever in view.

One morning I would drive back to Cooperstown. I would not plan it; I would simply invite Owen along. This might happen within a year, or two, or more. But if three decades elapsed and I still had not returned, then it would fall upon Julian or his new brother to invite me on a trip I might never have intended to take on my own.

Here is what Alison and I did on Owen's fourteenth birthday. After Julian left for school, we ambled west toward the Hudson. Alison moved more slowly now that she was eight months pregnant. At the corner of Sixth Avenue and Greenwich, we listened to a docent describe the house of detention that had stood on this spot until its destruction in 1973. The site is now occupied by a neighborhood garden we had never noticed.

We ate lunch in a small French restaurant on Tenth Avenue. Upon walking in, we recalled that we had celebrated Alison's thirty-fifth birthday there a few months before 9/11. In the afternoon, we ended up at the entrance of a gallery that was exhibiting photographs of watersheds, deltas, dry beds, irrigation sites, aquacultures, and mega-dams. The show made an argument about the sublime beauty and environmental costs of technology. A slight hesitation—and then we walked in.

In the evening, the rabbi who would officiate at the baby's circumcision met us at home. On the day of Owen's funeral, he had led an evening prayer outside, everyone assembled in a circle. Now the three of us sat in our living room and talked about the impending birth and Owen and also Julian, who came home from school as we wrapped things up. Julian did not join us on the couch, but he seemed pleased when we invited him to hold the baby during the ceremony.

Alison and I ended the day sitting side by side on our bed, feet planted on the floor. We talked about odds and ends—ordinary things on the least ordinary of days. Then Alison said something extraordinary, something that had never crossed my mind. Alison said she was relieved that Owen's birthday had come and gone without her giving birth. This prospect had been troubling her for months.

We sat and stared into the mirror a few feet away. Then I said, "It would have been unfair to the baby."

I cannot recall whether I framed this as a statement or a question, but Alison turned my way, her face soft and certain.

"No," she said. "It would have been unfair to Owen."

AUTHOR'S NOTE

This book rests on personal experiences and memories as well as letters, emails, diaries, speeches, photographs, and legal documents. These source materials cannot fill all gaps, however. Some things are bound to remain unknown. I have not invented anything though I did change a few names and biographical details to protect the privacy of individuals.

SOURCES

F ollowing Owen's death, I turned to literature and the past. The main sources I consulted, some of them mentioned in the book, are listed below.

GRIEF AND CHILDREN

Homer, *The Odyssey*, trans. Robert Fitzgerald (New York: Farrar, Straus and Giroux, 1998); Seneca, "To Marcia on Consolation," bit.ly/1qnPjco; Ben Jonson, "On My First Sone" (1603), poets.org/poetsorg/poem/my-first-son; *Letters to and from the Late Samuel Johnson*, 2 vols. (London: A. Strahan and T. Cadell, 1778); Victor Hugo, *Les Contemplations* (1856), in his *Oeuvres poétiques*, 3 vols., ed. Pierre Albouy (Paris: Gallimard, 1964–74), and *The Essential Victor Hugo*, trans. E. H. and A. M. Blackmore (Oxford: Oxford University Press, 1984); *The Poems of Emily Dickinson*, ed. R. W. Franklin (Cambridge, MA: Harvard University Press, 1999); Stéphane Mallarmé, *For Anatole's Tomb*, trans. Patrick McGuinness (Manchester: Carcanet, 2003 [first pub. 1961]) [I slightly amended this translation]; Georges Rodenbach, *Bruges-la-Morte* (Paris: GF-Flammarion, 1998 [first pub. 1892]); W. E. B. Du Bois, "Dawn of Mourning" (1899), reprinted in *Lapham's Quarterly* (Winter 2012), http://www.laphamsquarterly.org/family/dawn-mourning; Paul Gauguin, *Letters to His Wife and Friends*, trans. H. J. Stenning (Cleveland: World Publishing, 1949 [first pub. 1946]); Romain Rolland, *Journey Within* (New York: Philosophical Library, 1947 [first pub. 1942]); Philippe Forest, *Tous les enfants sauf un* (Paris: Gallimard, 2007); Annie Ernaux, *L'autre fille* (Paris: Nil, 2011).

I have reproduced a few lines from my *Nostradamus: How an Obscure Renaissance Astrologer Became the Modern Prophet of Doom* (New York: St. Martin's Press, 2012).

I also found evocative vignettes in Pat Jalland, *Death in the Victorian Family* (Oxford: Oxford University Press, 1996); Ginette Raimbault, *Lorsque l'enfant disparaît* (Paris: Odile Jacob, 1996); Julia-Marie Strange, *Death, Grief, and Poverty in Britain, 1870-1914* (Cambridge: Cambridge University Press, 2005); Drew Gilpin Faust, *This Republic of Suffering: Death and the American Civil War* (New York: Knopf, 2008); Jill Lepore, *The Mansion of Happiness: A History of Life and Death* (New York: Knopf, 2012).

BELARUS AND THE HOLOCAUST

Memorial Book of the Community of Bobruisk and Its Surroundings, ed. Y. Slutski (Tel-Aviv: Former Residents of Bobruisk in Israel and the U.S.A., 1967), 2 vols., online translation directed by David Gordon, http://www.jewishgen.org/yizkor/bobruisk/bysktoc1.html; *The Einsatzgruppen Reports: Selections from the Dispatches of the Nazi Death Squads' Campaign Against the Jews, July 1941-January 1943*, eds. Yitzhak Arad, Shmuel Krakowski, and Shmuel Spectors (New York: Holocaust Library, 1990); Samuel D. Kassow, *Who Will Write Our History? Rediscovering a Hidden Archive From the Warsaw Ghetto* (Bloomington: Indiana University Press, 2007 [repr. Vintage Books, 2009]); Barbara Epstein, *The Minsk Ghetto, 1941-1943: Jewish Resistance and Soviet Internationalism* (Berkeley: University of California Press, 2008); Timothy Snyder, "Holocaust: The Ignored Reality," *New York Review of Books*, July 16, 2009;

Yitzhak Arad, *The Holocaust in the Soviet Union* (Lincoln: University of Nebraska Press, 2009); Waitman Wade Beorn, *Marching into Darkness: The Wehrmacht and the Holocaust in Belarus* (Cambridge, MA: Harvard University Press, 2014).

THE GREEN RIVER

Literary and firsthand accounts. Washington Irving, *The Adventures of Captain Bonneville, U.S.A., in the Rocky Mountains and the Far West* (1859), in *Life and Works of Washington Irving* (New York: Pollard & Moss, 1882); E. O. Beaman, "The Cañon of the Colorado, and the Moquis Pueblos," *Appletons' Journal* 11 (April 25, 1874): 513–16; George T. Ferris, *Our Native Land: or, Glances at American Scenery and Places, With Sketches of Life and Adventure* (New York: D. Appleton, 1882); Theodore Roosevelt, *Ranch Life and the Hunting-Trail* (New York: Century, 1888); Ellsworth L. Kolb, *Through the Grand Canyon from Wyoming to Mexico* (New York: Macmillan, 1915); Ann Zwinger, *Run, River, Run: A Naturalist's Journey Down One of the Great Rivers of the American West* (Tucson: University of Arizona Press, 1975); Ellen Meloy, *Raven's Exile: A Season on the Green River* (New York: H. Holt, 1994); Alan Blackstock, ed., *A Green River Reader* (Salt Lake City: University of Utah Press, 2005).

John Wesley Powell's expeditions. Powell, *The Exploration of the Colorado River and Its Canyons,* introduced by Wallace Stegner (New York: Penguin, 1987 [first pub. 1874]); Frederick S. Dellenbaugh, *The Romance of the Colorado River: The Story of Its Discovery in 1540, With an Account of the Later Exploration* (New York: G. P. Putnam's Sons, 1909 [first pub. 1902]); Francis Marion Bishop, "Personal Reminiscences of John W. Powell," *Transactions of the Utah Academy of Sciences* 2 (1921): 16–27; Edward Dolnick, *Down the Great Unknown: John Wesley Powell's 1869 Journey of Discovery and Tragedy Through the Grand Canyon* (New York: HarperCollins,

2001); Donald Worster, *A River Running West: The Life of John Wesley Powell* (Oxford: Oxford University Press, 2001).

River runnings. Randall Henderson, "Boat Trip in the Canyon of Lodore," *The Desert Magazine* 19 (July 1956): 4–9; Colin Fletcher, *River: One Man's Journey Down the Colorado, Source to Sea* (New York: Random House, 1997); Roy Webb, ed., *High Wide and Handsome: The River Journals of Norman D. Nevills* (Logan, UT: Utah State University Press, 2005); "Green River Rafting Trip," August 10, 2006, Keseyscape blog, http://kesey.typepad.com/keseyscape/; Jeffrey St. Clair, "At Disaster Falls," *Counterpunch* (October 6–8, 2007), bit.ly/1UG9xdM; Roy Webb, *Riverman: The Story of Bus Hatch,* 3rd ed. (Flagstaff, AZ: Fretwater Press, 2008); Chris LeCheminant, "A Near Disaster in Disaster Falls," June 11, 2012, bit.ly/13F3h6h.

Guidebooks. G. E. Untermann and B. R. Untermann, *A Popular Guide to the Geology of Dinosaur National Monument* (Jensen, UT: Dinosaur Nature Association, 1969); Philip T. Hayes and George C. Simmons, *River Runner's Guide to Dinosaur National Monument and Vicinity* (Denver: Powell Society, 1973); William McGinnis, *Whitewater Rafting* (New York: Quadrangle/New York Times, 1975); Roderick Nash and Robert O. Collins, *The Big Drops: The Legendary Rapids of the American West,* rev. ed. (Boulder, CO: Johnson Books, 1989); Gary C. Nichols, *River Runner's Guide to Utah and Adjacent Areas,* rev. ed. (Salt Lake City: University of Utah Press, 2002); Carolyn Sutton, *The Family Guide to Colorado's National Parks and Monuments* (Englewood, CO: Westcliffe Publishers, 2006); Buzz Belknap and Loie Belknap Evans, *Belknap's Waterproof Dinosaur River Guide,* new ed. (Evergreen, CO: Westwater Books, 2008).

Newspapers. *Craig Daily Press, Los Angeles Times, Salt Lake Telegram, Vernal Express.*

ACKNOWLEDGMENTS

Alison and Julian allowed me to write a story that, while my own, is theirs as well. Before starting out, I told Alison there would be a great deal about her, as a real person but also, inevitably, as a character. It will be you, I explained, but only parts of you, filtered through my eyes. If Alison had expressed doubts, I would have shelved the project. But she told me to go ahead. There was nothing I could write, she said, that might make her ashamed.

When I told Julian, fourteen at the time, he asked if Alison knew and then urged me to write this book because it might avert other deaths on rafting trips. He also said that men rarely write about such things. A few years later, before leaving for college, he handed me personal notes and high school papers about the accident and its aftermath. He told me to use them as I saw fit. I demurred: what if he decided to write his own story one day? "If I do," Julian said, "it will be from a totally different place."

After all that happened, Alison and Julian trusted me to write this book. I may never fully convey how much this means.

For their openness and insights about this book, I am grateful to Annie Boland and Harry Fogarty; Catherine Cusset; Gay Block, Josh Gilbert, Dan Greenberg, Billie Parker, and Marie-Eve Thérenty; Elyssa Ackerman, Bart Everly, Laurie Gerson, Francine Gerson, Mitch Horowitz, Kathy Karp, Norm Magnusson, John Siciliano, Laura van Straaten, and Frédéric Viguier. Other friends proved generous in the last stretch: Dan Ain, Abbe Aronson, Claudia Baez, Craig Balsam, Mario Batali, Susi Cahn, Martha Frankel, Paul Katz, Sydney Mimeles, Jonathan van Meter, and Andy Young.

My agent, Steve Hanselman, and his wife, Julia Serebrinsky, championed *Disaster Falls* and immediately identified Rachel Klayman as the ideal editor. They were right. With empathy and intelligence and scrupulous attention to detail, Rachel helped me deepen the manuscript. Sometimes, she understood things before or even better than I did. Though I have published other books, I did not truly understand the craft of editing until I worked with Rachel. Meghan Houser also made profound contributions to the editorial process. Young but knowing, Meghan never let the nature of the material intimidate her. I am deeply indebted to both of them, as well as to Penny Simon, Danielle Crabtree, Jon Darga, and the entire team at Crown.

ABOUT THE AUTHOR

Stéphane Gerson is a cultural historian and Professor of French Studies at New York University. He has won several awards, including the Jacques Barzun Prize in Cultural History and the Laurence Wylie Prize in French Cultural Studies. He lives in Manhattan and Woodstock, New York, with his family.